Southwest Branch

NOV 12 2015

9010 35th Ave SW
Seattle, WA 98126

D0131893

'ERTY OF
LIBRARY

e v e r y d a y
PALEO
Thai Cuisine

authentic recipes made gluten-free

Victory Belt Publishing Inc.
Las Vegas

First Published in 2014 by Victory Belt Publishing Inc.

Copyright © 2014 Sarah Fragoso

All rights reserved. No part of this publication may be reproduced or distributed in any form or by any means, electronic or mechanical, or stored in a database or retrieval system, without prior written permission from the publisher.

ISBN 13: 978-1-628600-14-8

This book is for educational purposes. The publisher and author of this cookbook are not responsible in any manner whatsoever for any adverse effects arising directly or indirectly as a result of the information provided in this book.

Recipe and Travel Log Photos by Michael J. Lang, contact at michaeljlang@mac.com
Author Photo by Steve Twist

Printed in The USA
RRD0114

Contents

Introduction

Welcome to Everyday Paleo: Thai Cuisine. *I'm so excited to take you with me to Southeast Asia and share with you Thai cuisine! Food happens to be one of the most important elements of the culture that makes Thailand such a special gem in the world.*

I love Thai food.

"Love" is actually an understatement. The combination of sweet, savory, salty, and spicy; the smell of fresh kaffir lime, lemongrass, and galangal; the creaminess of coconut milk and the tartness of tamarind—they all make my heart sing with joy. My taste buds were built for Thai cuisine, and it's the culinary foundation for many of the dishes on my blog and in my other books.

This book is the real deal—all the recipes come straight from my experiences in Thailand and what I learned while traveling throughout the country. At the same time, I've made sure they're all Paleo-friendly; you will find recipes that include white rice or rice noodles, but I always provide substitutions if you do not eat rice. (I explain my stance on rice on page 22.) In the next chapter, you will find a detailed account of the ingredients that I suggest you use and why.

While in Thailand, I was able to cook with people from different regions, backgrounds, and experiences, and their combined influence is what made this book a reality. The hours and hours of cooking, photographing, tasting, and testing that made this book come together were all possible thanks to the time that the gracious people of Thailand gave me on my travels through their great country.

Thai Kitchen Essentials: The Ingredients and Tools of Thai Cuisine

Please, dear readers, do not skip this section of the book and fly right to the actual recipes. I understand the temptation, believe me! I often read cookbooks that way, too—I want to get right to the "meat and potatoes" of the book (if you'll pardon the pun) and start cooking. But the following paragraphs will give you an understanding of Thai food that you'll find helpful when making these recipes: which ingredients are necessary, what substitutions you can use, which tools are essential, and where you can find certain products. I want to make sure you have the best experience possible while using this book, so please take the time to read this chapter.

Thank you, and enjoy!

What Sets
Thai Food
Apart

Thai food is special—period. Creating the flavors of Thailand requires particular ingredients and an understanding of what makes Thai food . . . well, Thai food. One of the first things I learned in Thailand is that when you're cooking Thai food, the goal is to achieve a balance of flavors among spicy, sour, sweet, salty, and (sometimes) bitter. I admit, I often questioned if "spicy" is really in balance in traditional Thai food, because it is hot*—but yes, the balance is always there, and, speaking as a Westerner who loves spicy food, my culinary Thai trip brought my understanding of spicy to an entirely different level. The beauty of Thai food is that it is up to you, as the cook in your kitchen, to determine what kind of flavor balance you want to achieve with each dish.*

Most Thai dishes combine four essential items: protein, seasoning, vegetable or filler, and the key ingredients. The key ingredients are what gives a dish its identity. For example, if you make tom yum goong (a creamy hot and sour prawn soup) with regular ginger instead of galangal, what you have is something that is kind of like tom yum goong but is not what tom yum goong should be. Nusi, the owner of a cooking school in Bangkok, was the first Thai chef to tell me this, and the idea makes perfect sense. It goes along with the idea of the balance of flavors. Thai food is not always the same, nor is one person's recipe exactly like another's, but Thai food is precise, which is why there are always key ingredients in every recipe. You may have noticed just by eating at different Thai restaurants that a dish like Tom Ka Gai (Sweet and Sour Coconut and Chicken Soup, page 158), for example, might taste different at each establishment, but the key ingredients are always constant—the floating pieces of kaffir lime leaves, galangal, and lemongrass are what make the soup what it is, even if the soup at one location might be just a bit sweeter or more sour than at the next location.

In America, a hamburger is a hamburger, no matter what kind of spice rub or sauce you add on. Not so with Thai food. Pad thai is rice noodles with spices and tamarind paste, which gives it that special sourness, along with a bit of sugar. Substitute lime juice for tamarind paste? Sure! But it's no longer pad thai—it resembles it, but it's not the real deal. Does that mean you should forgo making substitutions in any recipe in this book? Absolutely not! But understand that you are making a variation on the true, authentic recipe.

The recipes in this book will give you a framework for what makes each dish what it is, but it's entirely up to you to change the important components or key ingredients to suit your taste. It's usually possible to change the protein or filler and still achieve a result similar to what the recipe calls for, but if you change the key ingredients or seasoning, you will not always achieve what you might expect. However, this doesn't mean that you shouldn't experiment with the balance of flavors. You might want ten chiles in your dish while I might want only two, or you might like a bit more sweetness in your stir-frys than your neighbor does. Cooking Thai food means experimenting and tasting as you cook; I can't stress that enough, and it's important to have your seasoning ingredients close at hand so you can add a little more as needed, building the flavors rather than simply trusting to exact measurements. These recipes are a guide, not a Thai food bible with rules that have to be followed exactly.

Finally, we need to discuss how a Thai meal is eaten. Thai food is meant to be shared, and in Thailand, when people gather together, several dishes are prepared, typically more dishes than there are people, and everyone eats a little bit of each dish. It's what we might call "family style" here in America. Because of this tradition, the recipes in this book will make enough to serve two to three people, so if you want to make only one dish for a family of five, for example, you will need to double or triple the amounts given in the recipe.

So with that, I invite you to explore, taste, create, and most importantly, have fun! Throw a few Thai food parties, and as always, enjoy.

Thai Ingredients, Substitutions, and Kitchen Tools

Let's take a little culinary trip to Thailand together and I'll share with you the special Thai ingredients that are used throughout the recipes, where to find them, and, if you can't find them, what you can use as a substitute.

Fresh Herbs and Vegetables

Basil

Basil has been a staple ingredient in Thai cooking for over four thousand years. Several types of basil are found in Thailand, and different varieties are used for different dishes, depending on the desired flavor. Here are the most common varieties:

1. **Sweet Thai basil:** Closest to the basil commonly used in the West

2. **Holy basil:** Very pungent, with a lemony scent and a peppery flavor

3. **Lemon basil:** Very strong lemony scent and more mild and delicate flavor than holy basil

Basil is typically either served fresh or added at the end of the cooking time because cooking basil for too long destroys the delicate flavor. If you're not using the entire leaf, it's better to tear the leaves than cut them.

Most of these Thai varieties of basil can be found at farmers markets, specialty grocers, and Asian markets.

Substitutions: You can substitute the standard basil that's commonly found in grocery stores for all the varieties listed above.

Thai Chiles

There are about seventy-nine varieties of chiles in Thailand, but I'll introduce to you just the ones you will be using most often with this book. The heat of Thai chiles generally depends on their size: small chiles are the hottest and the largest chiles are the mildest. The recipes here call for small, medium, or large chiles rather than identifying them by name, and really, whatever chiles you can find locally will work.

Here's what to look for:

1. Small red or green chiles, also known as **red or green bird's eye chiles**
2. Medium red or green chiles, also known as **spur chiles**
3. Large red or green chiles, also known as large **cayenne peppers**
4. **Dried chiles** (large, medium, and small)

Substitutions: Any hot chiles will work for the recipes that call for chiles. Red habaneros, jalapeños, Fresno peppers, or serranos can be used when small and medium chiles are called for—just start with a little bit and add more according to your heat tolerance. You can also use jalapeños or New Mexico chiles for large chiles, but typically you can find small Thai or bird's eye chiles as well as cayenne and spur chiles at most Asian markets, or even at large grocery stores that have a good produce department.

Dried chiles are easy to find in most Asian markets and in the Latino section of major grocery stores. Chiles de árbol are the smaller and spicier dried chiles, guajillo chiles are medium-sized and spicy, and Anaheim chiles are the larger dried chiles and are not quite as spicy.

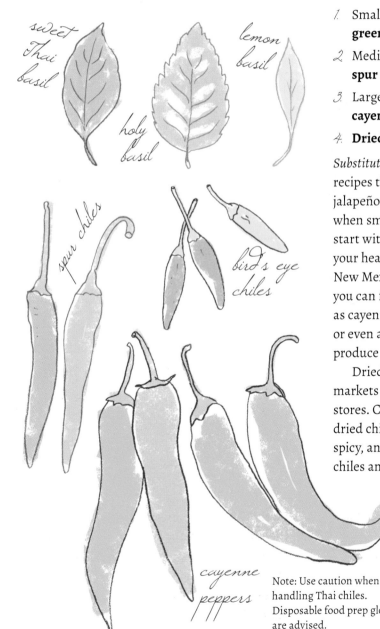

sweet Thai basil

holy basil

lemon basil

spur chiles

bird's eye chiles

cayenne peppers

dried chiles

Note: Use caution when handling Thai chiles. Disposable food prep gloves are advised.

Chinese Celery

Chinese celery has a stronger flavor than the celery we are used to, and it has very thin stems and an abundance of leaves. This herb is almost always cooked, although now and then you'll see it called for in a salad.

Substitutions: When a recipe calls for Chinese celery, you can substitute regular celery; just try to use the leafy ends when possible.

Chinese Ginger/Fingerroot

This member of the ginger family is much harder to find outside of Southeast Asia than its cousin, galangal. This thin, finger-like spice can often be found pickled; if you use pickled Chinese ginger, just make sure to soak it in water for a few minutes and rinse it well before using.

Substitutions: Regular ginger may be substituted for Chinese ginger.

Chinese celery

Chinese ginger/fingerroot

cilantro/coriander

Chinese shallots

Chinese Shallots

When a recipe in this book calls for shallots, it's referring to the smaller Chinese shallots that are common throughout Southeast Asia. You can of course use the shallots that we are used to seeing here in the West, but if possible, try to find actual Chinese shallots!

Substitutions: Use regular shallots or red onions as a substitute for Chinese shallots.

Cilantro/Coriander

Coriander is better known in North America by its Spanish name, cilantro, though that usually refers only to the leaves. The Thais typically use the root for making curry paste or adding depth of flavor to other dishes. You can often find cilantro with the roots still attached at farmers markets or Asian markets. Like basil, this herb is typically added at the end of the cooking time to maintain its delicate flavor, and it's used most often as a garnish.

Substitutions: Cilantro is usually easy to find at any major grocery store. If a recipe calls for the root of the plant but you are unable to find it with the root still on, you can substitute the cilantro stems.

Eggplant

This vegetable is very different in Thailand than what we are used to finding in the States. Two varieties are commonly used in these recipes:

1. **Pea eggplant:** This is the most commonly used eggplant in Thai cooking, and it looks just as you'd expect: like a large green pea. It's bitter when eaten raw, but the bitterness decreases once cooked.

2. **Thai eggplant:** About the size of a small apple or golf ball, this eggplant is softer and sweeter in flavor than the pea eggplant, and it stays a bit crunchy when you cook it.

Substitutions: If you can't find the kind of eggplant the recipe calls for, you can use a small Japanese eggplant or any other eggplant variety that's available in your area.

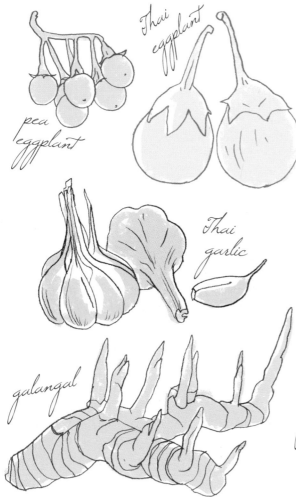

Galangal

Although it's a member of the ginger family, galangal has a unique smell, flavor, and texture. The flesh of galangal is creamy on the inside and light brown with sometimes a purple hue on the outside. Its skin is much thinner than that of regular ginger. Galangal, like lemongrass and kaffir lime leaves, is typically used to flavor a dish, but sometimes it's also eaten.

Substitutions: It's often easy to find dried galangal in the ethnic aisle of your grocery store, but fresh galangal may be found in your local Asian market; other sources are listed in the resources guide at the end of the chapter. If you use dried galangal, be sure to reconstitute it by soaking in water prior to using it. I do not recommend using powdered galangal. You can also substitute regular ginger for galangal—it will not lend the dish the special flavor of true galangal, but it will still be delicious.

Thai Garlic

Thai garlic has a pink tinge to its skin. It's spicier than the garlic we are used to but also has a sweeter flavor. When cooking with Thai garlic, you do not have to peel away the skin that is closest to the flesh of the garlic clove—it's usually cooked or pounded into curry pastes right along with the clove of the garlic.

Substitutions: Any garlic that you can find locally can be substituted for Thai garlic.

Ginger

This is simply common ginger, which is easy to find in most major grocery stores and is most often cooked with meats and in curries to add flavor.

Kaffir Lime

The kaffir lime is a small, bumpy, warty fruit that has a very strong citrus smell. It's too acidic to eat, but the rind is used to make curry pastes or to flavor other dishes with its zest. The kaffir lime is used most often for medicinal or household purposes. The skin of the fruit, for example, is used in tonics to aid digestion, and you'll often see the limes lying about, cut open, in Thai homes as an air freshener. The juice can also be used as a cleanser for clothes, and the oil can be added to shampoos or used as a hair rinse. When you use the rind of the kaffir lime, be sure to not use the pith; it's very bitter and should be avoided.

Substitutions: As with the kaffir lime leaves, there is truly no good substitute for this special ingredient. It's worth ordering online if you are unable to find it locally. If you must, you can use the rind or zest from a regular lime instead, but it won't come close to achieving the same flavor enhancement as the treasured kaffir lime.

Lemongrass

This awesome ingredient gives soups, curry pastes, and salads an unequivocal lemony taste that can only come from lemongrass. Usually the tough outer layer of the grass must be removed before you can get down to where the grass is tender enough to cut. When it's used as a flavoring for soups, the lemongrass is not intended for consumption. Several recipes, including those for curry paste, call for lemongrass to be pounded into a paste or finely sliced, and only with these preparations should it be eaten. When it's left in large pieces at least 1 inch long, it's only used to add flavor. You can often find lemongrass at most major grocery stores or health food stores that have a good produce department, and of course at most Asian markets.

Substitutions: If you absolutely cannot find lemongrass, the best substitute is lemon zest or lemon leaves; however, let me stress that it's worth hunting down.

kaffir lime

lemongrass

kaffir lime leaves

Kaffir Lime Leaves

The leaf of the kaffir lime is a truly special ingredient that's unique to Thai cooking. It has a strong and delightful citrus smell that is released when the leaf is torn or bruised. Make sure you always remove the tough stem from the leaves before using. When kaffir lime leaves are torn and added to soups and curries, they are for flavor only—they're too big and fibrous to be eaten. However, the leaves are intended to be eaten when they're chiffonaded (thinly sliced). You can find kaffir lime leaves at Asian markets; other resources are listed at the end of this chapter.

Substitutions: I hate to say it, but after consulting with several of my Thai friends, I haven't found a really good substitute for the adored kaffir lime leaf. The good news is that you can order this wonderful ingredient online (see the resources at the end of this section), and the leaves freeze beautifully and can be kept for several months in a plastic bag. It's totally worth making the online purchase! If you absolutely must, you can substitute the zest of one lime for every two kaffir lime leaves.

Long Beans

Long beans are similar in taste and texture to the classic green bean and are eaten both raw and cooked in several Thai dishes. Long beans do not store well, so if you find them at your local farmers market or grocery store, plan on using them within the first day or two of buying them.

Substitutions: Green beans are a totally acceptable substitute for long beans.

Mushrooms

In Thailand there are several varieties of mushrooms; the most commonly used are straw mushrooms, which are small, light brown mushrooms that have a meaty texture and a smooth surface. Shiitake mushrooms, which are easier to find in the U.S., are also used, as are ear mushrooms, which are big, flat, thin, and dark.

Substitutions: For any of these mushrooms, you can substitute white, button, or crimini mushrooms, which can all be found in any major grocery store.

long beans

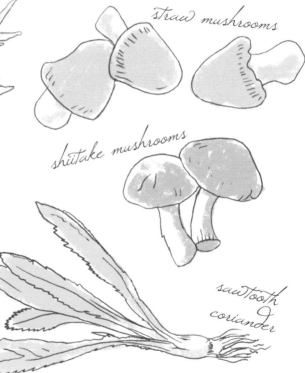

straw mushrooms

shiitake mushrooms

sawtooth coriander

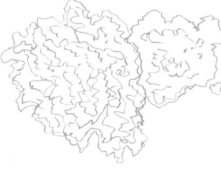

Dried snow mushrooms

Dried Snow Mushrooms

These are used in one of the salad recipes in this book and are absolutely divine. You can find dried snow mushrooms in most Asian markets and sometimes in the ethnic aisle of major grocery stores.

Substitutions: You could use white, button, or crimini mushrooms instead, but the flavor, consistency, and texture will be very different—though still tasty!

Sawtooth Coriander

This herb smells and tastes very similar to its cousin, cilantro; however, sawtooth coriander looks very different and has a much stronger flavor. You can sometimes find this herb at farmers markets or at your local Asian market.

Substitutions: Regular cilantro works just fine as a substitute for sawtooth coriander.

Stink Beans

Stink beans, whose Thai name is *sataw*, are commonly found in southern Thai cuisine. True to their name, stink beans emit an odd odor, but despite the smell they have a surprisingly benign and almost nutty flavor. Stink beans are difficult to find in the U.S., but sometimes you can find them frozen or pickled in Asian markets. The frozen beans can be used in stir-frys, but the pickled ones are usually eaten on their own with chili sauce.

Substitutions: Green beans are a great substitution for stink beans—they're easier to find, have no smell, and are more palatable for Western taste buds.

Turmeric

Another member of the ginger family, this root is used in curry pastes. You'll find its powdered form called for in a few recipes in this book. The bright color and mild flavor adds a wonderful accent and visual appeal to a dish.

Substitutions: If you cannot find fresh turmeric, you can substitute powdered turmeric, which is easily found in the spice section of all major grocery stores.

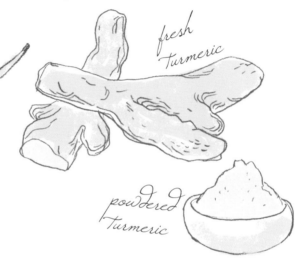

stink beans

fresh turmeric

powdered turmeric

Seasonings

Fish Sauce

Fish sauce is a seasoning made from fermented anchovies, and although it sounds awful, it's what gives the umami flavor to most Thai dishes.

Oyster Sauce

This is an important ingredient that adds a slightly salty and sweet taste to several dishes, including stir-frys, noodle dishes, and fried rice. I have only been able to find one gluten-free bottled oyster sauce, Wok Mei, but I have provided a recipe to make your own (page 58)! The Wok Mei oyster sauce does contain some cornstarch as a thickening agent, but the taste is good and it's much easier to buy it than make your own. However, if you are very sensitive to cornstarch or want to avoid it altogether, I recommend going the homemade route.

Dried Shrimp

This is a key ingredient in many of the salads in this book and adds a little bit of salty, yummy crunch to many dishes. You can find dried shrimp in Asian markets or online, and it can be stored in the refrigerator for several months.

Shrimp Paste

This is an essential ingredient in many southern Thai dishes and curry pastes. The smell is overpowering and pungent—which is to be expected, since it's made from shrimp that has been fermented with salt in the heat and humidity of Southeast Asia. However, like fish sauce, once it's mixed with other ingredients, it provides a unique and wonderful taste.

Soy Sauce

A staple seasoning agent. But instead of regular soy sauce, I recommend using coconut aminos, which are made from fermented coconut sap and are entirely soy- and gluten-free. If you can tolerate some fermented soy product, you can also substitute wheat-free tamari for regular soy sauce, which often contains wheat and therefore is not always gluten-free.

Tamarind

Tamarind pods can be found at most Asian markets; other sources are listed in the resources guide at the end of the chapter. The method for preparing tamarind paste from tamarind pods can be found on page 44. Tamarind is used for its sourness, and its unique flavor profile can be found in many Thai dishes.

Substitutions: You can substitute coconut vinegar or rice vinegar for tamarind paste, but use half the recommended amount and then add more as needed for the desired flavor.

tamarind pods

Rice and Rice Noodles

Many Thai recipes call for rice or noodles. Rice is naturally gluten-free, and white rice tends to be less problematic for folks than other grains because the outer shell, which contains most of the nutrients that might be irritating to the gut, has been stripped away. Rice is a staple ingredient in Thailand, and most of the noodles are made of rice flour, not wheat flour.

Most people who eat Paleo try to avoid rice, but many seem to do just fine incorporating some white rice into their real-food diets. My family eats white rice without much issue, so we tend to incorporate it as a healthy "safe starch" now and then. I sometimes use white rice in place of cauliflower rice for the fried rice recipes found in this book, and occasionally I use rice noodles for Pad Thai (Stir-Fried Rice

Noodles, page 120) and Pad See Ew (Stir-Fried Flat Noodles, page 122), and in some of the soup recipes as well. I do always offer an alternative if you would like to avoid rice and all rice products completely, but otherwise feel free to use white rice or rice noodles. However, if you have an autoimmune condition or a fat-loss goal, I recommend avoiding rice and other rice products altogether.

The kinds of rice most commonly found in Thailand are jasmine rice (page 36) and sticky or glutinous rice (page 38). Glutinous rice has nothing to do with gluten; it's naturally gluten-free. The name comes from the fact that it becomes more "glue-like" or sticky when cooked.

Palm Sugar and Suggested Alternatives

Thai food is made of a balance of flavors, and "sweet" is one of those flavors—it's one of the things that make Thai food, Thai food. Please remember, it's up to you entirely to make your dishes as sweet as you want them to be. The amounts given in the recipes are merely a guide that you can tweak and adjust to meet your needs. As someone who's trying to follow a whole-food diet, I generally avoid sugar, but the small amount of sweeteners that are called for in these recipes are not what you would find in a treat; most often only a couple of teaspoons are required to achieve the desired balance of flavors.

That said, I want to discuss the types of sweeteners that I recommend in these recipes and explain why I will not ask you to use palm sugar, even though it's traditionally used in most Thai dishes. Some argue that the production of palm sugar—and coconut sugar, for that matter—is not sustainable and that we should avoid palm sugar and coconut sugar, which are being hyped as the next "healthy sugars." Because the flower is harvested from the coconut tree to make the sugar, it hinders the tree from producing coconuts. Those opposed to using or supporting the use of palm sugar and coconut sugar are also concerned about the ethical practices associated with the production of these items.

Although these practices may have changed by the time you read this, because of what I know today, I feel better recommending tried-and-true, more sustainable, and close-to-nature sweeteners: maple syrup and honey. The flavor of maple syrup especially is very similar to palm sugar, and it's easy for anyone to find a high-quality maple syrup.

In my opinion, there is no such thing as "healthy sugar," but some options are better than others, and it's most important to make sure your sweetener comes straight from nature and is sustainably sourced. If you are worried about using any sort of sweetener, you can always choose to omit it, or consider substituting an equal amount of organic, unfiltered pineapple or apple juice.

Cooking Oils for Stir-Frying and Deep-Frying

Thai food is all about stir-frying and deep-frying, which are both a lot of fun. In Thailand, the cooking oil of choice used to be animal fat or palm oil. Unfortunately, as Western and other Asian countries begin to make their influence felt in Thailand, the cooking oil of choice is becoming, more often than not, soybean oil. Palm oil is still commonly used and easy to find in Thailand, but I'm not very confident in the quality of the oil or the ethical practices associated with its harvesting and production. The good news is that a lot of smaller farms and operations in Thailand are now demanding or producing palm oil that's made in a sustainable, ethical way.

Here are the types of oils I recommend

Palm Shortening

This is, by far, my favorite product to use for deep-frying. Palm shortening has a very high smoke point, does not have any flavor, and will not splatter as readily as coconut oil. Furthermore, palm shortening is not prone to rancidity and can be reused. I purchase palm shortening and virgin palm oil only from Tropical Traditions, which gets its oil from a small farm in West Africa that supports sustainable practices and not from the palm oil giants in Southeast Asia, which have questionable practices.

Leaf Lard

Leaf lard is also an excellent choice for stir-frying and deep-frying, but because the price point is a bit higher, I still prefer palm shortening, especially for deep-frying.

Coconut Oil

I recommend using coconut oil for stir-frying but not for deep-frying. Although coconut oil is fairly stable at high heat, using it for deep-frying can cause significant splattering, and the desired crispiness is harder to obtain. Stick to fast stir-frys for coconut oil and you will love the subtle flavor that it adds to your already delicious dishes.

Virgin Palm Oil

Palm oil is fun to experiment with for your stir-frys, but high-quality palm oil does leave everything a little bit red, and it has a rich flavor that I enjoy but that you should try before you commit to using it all the time. Virgin palm oil has a very high smoke point and you can deep-fry with it.

Deep-fry skimmer

Cooking and Prepping Tools

Cheesecloth or Nut Milk Bag

This tool is the key to successful homemade coconut milk, and you can also use it to dive into the world of homemade almond milk. A cheesecloth is also necessary for making Sticky Rice (page 38).

Coconut Shredder, Cracker, and Demeater

These handy tools will be immensely helpful if you decide to make homemade coconut milk. See page 32 for detailed instructions on how to accomplish this very gratifying task.

Deep-Fry Skimmer

Keeping it simple is super important, and with a deep-fry skimmer, you'll look like a pro scooping deep-fried fish or bananas out of hot oil. Plus— and more important—it's much less painful than using your fingers.

Food Processor/Blender/Vitamix

Most people already own a food processor or blender, and yes, you can absolutely use one to make your curry pastes. A Vitamix is the most effective tool besides the traditional mortar and pestle because of its ability to grind up just about anything! However, as mentioned in the mortar and pestle descriptions, when you use a modern method you lose some of the intensity of the flavors that enhance all Thai dishes. That said, I have made curry pastes both ways, and no one but an experienced Thai food critic would truly be able to tell the difference. However, I still strongly recommend that you make food processors and blenders your second choice, after the authentic mortar and pestle.

Grater

In Thai salads, the vegetables and fruits are often grated. For example, in Som Tum (Papaya Salad, page 92), a green papaya is grated and then mixed and mashed with the other ingredients to help incorporate its flavor and juices with each component of the dish.

cheesecloth

blender

nut milk bag

grater

coconut demeater

coconut shredder

Granite Mortar and Pestle

During our travels through Thailand, I heard a story about how Thai men used to find a wife, back when everyone still used a mortar and pestle to grind their curry pastes. When coming home from the fields, they would listen for the obvious noise of a mortar and pestle being used in the kitchens they passed. Based on how loud the noise was, they would know how strong a woman was, how good her curry paste would taste, and how quickly dinner would be done! Today, most people in Thailand buy their curry pastes premade from the market, but many still keep tradition alive by making their own at home with a mortar and pestle. Several people told me that if I were to attempt my own curry pastes at home, this was absolutely the way to do it. A granite mortar and pestle is used traditionally in Thailand; the granite has enough weight to break down the tough, fibrous ingredients that make curry paste, such as lemongrass and galangal, and whole spices like peppercorns and coriander seeds. Also, granite helps to keep the ingredients cool, preventing them from oxidizing, and it won't affect the flavor of the curry. I recommend using an 8-inch granite mortar and pestle.

Wooden or Earthenware Mortar and Pestle

Wooden or earthenware mortar and pestles are used for making more delicate dishes like Som Tum (Papaya Salad, page 92) or Som Tum Taeng Lao (Spicy Cucumber Salad, page 96). You can also use a wooden mortar and pestle to create pastes with garlic cloves and Thai chiles, which form the base for many stir-frys and soups. Pounding ingredients rather than mincing or chopping them changes a dish's flavor because of the way in which the fibers are broken down. When garlic and chiles are pounded together, the flavor is better distributed throughout the dish and is less dissipated and more intact. The end result will still be good if you forgo using a mortar and pestle, but you will be missing out on a part of Thai food that is truly authentic and unique. I strongly suggest you make a mortar and pestle a part of your kitchen arsenal.

Saucepan

A good saucepan is such a great tool to have, especially for all the yummy condiments and sauces that you will find in this book!

Soup Pot

There are quite a few soup recipes in this book, and you can also make curries in a soup pot. However, if you don't have a soup pot, you can often use a wok for both as well.

wooden mortar and pestle

granite mortar and pestle

saucepan

soup pot

Splatter Guard

Please do not e-mail me to tell me that you burned yourself while making Moo Krob Kua Klau (Stir-Fried Crispy Pork Belly, page 178) or Cap Moo (Pork Rinds, page 90) only to later reveal that you attempted these recipes without using a splatter guard. Deep-frying is fun but accidents can happen easily, so please, before you attempt any of the deep-fried deliciousness in this book, get a splatter guard!

Vegetable Spiralizer

Rice noodles, which are gluten-free, are a common ingredient in Thai cooking. For folks who are otherwise healthy, do not have an autoimmune disease, and do not have a fat-loss goal, rice noodles may be a good addition to your whole-foods diet, and you can use them whenever a recipe calls for noodles. But if you prefer to avoid rice and rice products altogether, the best substitute is vegetable "noodles" made with a vegetable spiralizer. With this amazing tool, you can make noodles out of anything, from sweet potatoes to zucchini, and I highly recommend having one around. As a bonus, your kids will love it, and you'll see their vegetable consumption ratchet up a notch thanks to this handy gadget.

Wok

The majority of Thai dishes are made in a wok. Ovens are not used at all in traditional Thai cooking, and it's way too hot in Thailand to turn on an oven anyway. Most cooking is done outside over an open flame. If something is to be "roasted"—usually herbs and spices or onions and garlic—it's typically done in a dry wok. You will find one recipe in this book in which I recommend roasting chiles and onions in the oven, which you will thank me for; sometimes our modern conveniences are just easier. However, you really do want to invest in a good wok. Thai cooking is done fast over high heat, and a wok has a nifty way of transferring the heat from the flame evenly over the surface. Plus, the bowl shape is great for tossing and stirring as you quickly stir-fry meat and delicate vegetables. I also like to deep-fry right in my cast iron wok. With its wide mouth, it's easier to scoop out food from the hot oil, and with a splatter guard, you can protect yourself and keep your kitchen somewhat grease-free.

vegetable spiralizer

splatter guard

wok

Resource Guide

Now that we've discussed all the nifty ingredients and tools you'll need in order to get the full experience of Thai cuisine, let's talk about where to find all this great stuff. If you have an Asian market in your town, start there. Bring your list of goodies and see what they can help you with. Often, Asian markets have local suppliers who specialize in growing items like lemongrass, and shopping there is a great opportunity to support your local economy. However, depending on where you live, it might be impossible to find some of the required ingredients. While I've listed possible substitutes in the previous section, if you want the real deal, there are online stores where you can order just about everything you will need to make each dish truly authentic.

Recommended Brands*

Curry paste: Mae Ploy

Fish sauce: Red Boat

Shrimp paste: Tra Chang

Coconut aminos: Coconut Secret

Coconut oil: Tropical Traditions

Palm oil / palm shortening: Tropical Traditions

Leaf lard: Fatworks

Oyster sauce: Wok Mei (although gluten-free, it does include non-GMO cornstarch, cane syrup, caramel color, and maltodextrin)

Lee Kum Kee Panda Brand Green Label (harder to find than Wok Mei, it has the same basic ingredients)

Maple syrup / raw organic honey / organic whole sugar: Tropical Traditions

Coconut milk: Native Forest

Where to Order*

ImportFood.com

In my opinion, this is the best resource for all the Thai ingredients, mortars and pestles, woks, and deep-fry skimmers that you will ever need. Their produce is fresh, delivery is prompt, and shipping costs are reasonable. They also carry Mae Ploy brand curry paste, which is the highest quality premade curry paste that I have found—it has no MSG, soybean oil, or other vegetable oils or preservatives, only the true ingredients of curry paste and a very fresh taste that will not disappoint. Also, look for Tra Chang shrimp paste, which has no additives, just shrimp and salt—the only ingredients true shrimp paste should ever have. Finally, ImportFood.com has every fresh ingredient, from lemongrass to kaffir limes, needed to make the authentic versions of the recipes in this book.

GroceryThai (www.grocerythai.com)

With everything from authentic coconut graters to woks to fresh produce, this site has it all!

Young Coconuts (www.youngcoconuts.com)

This is the place to order all your coconut-cracking, shredding, and demeating tools. These are a must if you decide to make coconut milk the traditional way, with mature coconuts rather than coconut flakes. (Instructions for making coconut milk are found on page 32.)

Amazon.com

Yes, good old Amazon really can come through! You can find woks, nut milk bags, cheesecloth, deep-frying tools, and even my recommended brand of curry pastes, coconut milk, and oyster sauces on Amazon.

Tropical Traditions (www.tropicaltraditions.com)

Here you can find sustainably produced coconut oil, virgin palm oil, palm shortening, maple syrup, honey, whole cane sugar, and coconut vinegar.

Coconut Secret (www.coconutsecret.com)

If you can't find coconut aminos in your local health food store or grocery store, this is the place to order them.

Fatworks (www.fatworksfoods.com)

The most trusted source for all things animal fat, such as their amazing leaf lard, which is wonderful for deep-frying and stir-frying!

Please note, I have not received any compensation for these recommendations. These brands are merely my favorites based on ingredients, quality, and taste.

Essentials, Condiments, and Curry Pastes

Coconut Milk

Nam Kati

Traditional Thai coconut milk is made from mature coconut meat, and the process is definitely not easy. I learned how to make fresh coconut milk and coconut cream from Nusi, but we purchased pre-grated mature coconut from the market. You can sometimes find fresh, raw, grated coconut in the freezer section of an Asian market. If you can't find pre-grated fresh coconut, follow the steps below to make traditional coconut milk. I've also provided an easier method that uses dried coconut flakes, but I suggest attempting the traditional method at least once to get the full experience.

Thai people usually make fresh coconut milk every day and use what they make that same day. You can, however, keep fresh coconut milk in an airtight glass container in the refrigerator for 3 to 4 days. You can also freeze it in a glass mason jar; just fill it about three-quarters full and let it freeze before putting on the airtight lid (this will keep the glass from breaking when it freezes). It takes a while to thaw coconut milk, so allow a day to defrost it in the refrigerator.

Prep time using fresh coconut: 30 minutes

Prep time using coconut flakes: 5 minutes

Yield: Around 2 cups

1. Use a screwdriver to punch a hole into the soft "eye" of two mature coconuts. The eye is found on one end and looks like three dark spots, and punching a hole there lets the water drain and decreases the mess.

2. Crack open both coconuts by hitting the center with the dull side of a cleaver, a large knife, or hammer until the coconut cracks.

3. Using a paring knife or a coconut demeater (shown on page 25), carefully cut out large chunks of coconut.

4. Grate the coconut meat. You can do this with a handheld grater or food processor (make sure you use the grating blade).

5. Place the grated coconut in a large bowl and add enough warm water to just cover it. Use your hands to massage and squeeze the coconut for several minutes, until the water turns white and creamy. You now have coconut cream.

6. Pour the coconut cream through a sieve to strain out the coconut flakes.

7. Return the same coconut flakes to the bowl, add warm water, and repeat the process. The second time around, the liquid will not be quite as creamy. Strain the liquid through a sieve, and now you have coconut milk.

1.

2.

3.

4.

5.

6.

Alternately, you can place the coconut flakes in a food processor or blender, add just enough water to cover the flakes (usually about 4 cups), and pulse until smooth. The result will be thick and creamy, like a milkshake.

Pour the contents of the blender or food processor into a cheesecloth or a nut milk bag and carefully squeeze and strain the liquid into a bowl. Tada! Fresh coconut milk!

If you are unable to find fresh coconuts or want to avoid the hassle, here is an easier way to make coconut milk at home.

Place 3 cups of dried unsweetened coconut flakes in a food processor or blender. Add 3 cups of hot (not boiling) water and pulse until smooth.

Strain through a cheesecloth or nut milk bag. There you have it: fresh coconut milk!

You can reuse the coconut flakes left behind in the nut milk bag or cheesecloth by making them into coconut flour. Just dehydrate them and grind the dried flakes into a flour-like consistency in a food processor. You can also use the leftover coconut flakes in the recipe for Khao Koor (Toasted Rice Powder, page 46).

Jasmine Rice

Khao Hom Mali

Jasmine rice differs from long grain white rice in its nutty flavor and floral scent. Jasmine rice is the most common rice found in Thai cooking, and you will love its delicate taste and fluffy texture. The easiest way to prepare jasmine rice is with a rice cooker. Simply follow the manufacturer's instructions, turn it on, and walk away. If you do not have a rice cooker, the following directions will always result in perfectly cooked rice.

One cup of uncooked rice yields about 3 ½ cups of cooked rice, which is enough to feed two to three people. To feed more, double or triple the amounts of water and rice.

Prep time: 5 minutes
Cook time: Approximately 20 minutes
Serves: 2 to 3

1 cup jasmine rice
1 1/2 cups cold water

Place the rice in a sieve and rinse under cool water until the water is no longer cloudy.

Add the rinsed rice to a pot and cover with the cold water.

Bring to a boil over high heat, then turn the heat down to low and cover.

Let the rice simmer, covered, for approximately 15 minutes, or until the rice has soaked up all of the water.

Remove from heat and let sit, still covered, for an additional 5 minutes.

Uncover and fluff with a fork before serving.

Sticky Rice

Khao Niao

Sticky rice, also called "glutinous rice," is soaked and then steamed, not simmered in water. It's referred to as "sticky rice" because the end result is just that—it sticks together and has a unique sticky consistency. It's sometimes also referred to as "sweet rice" because this particular variety of rice has a naturally sweeter taste. Soaking the rice first is imperative in making sticky rice; otherwise, you will end up with hard rice.

You will need a steamer to make sticky rice, and an actual sticky rice steamer with a bamboo basket is best. While you can make it without one, it's difficult to get the correct distance between the water and the rice. You will also need a cheesecloth.

Prep time: 2 hours or overnight to soak the rice

Cook time: 10 minutes

Serves: 2

1 cup uncooked sticky rice

1 to 1 1/2 cups cold water

Place the rice in a sieve and rinse under cold water, using your hands to move the rice around. Rinse until the water starts to run clear.

Place the rinsed rice in a bowl, cover with more cold water, and let soak for at least 2 hours or overnight.

Drain the rice.

Add the water to the bottom of your rice steamer. The water should be no more than 5 inches from the bottom of the steamer.

Place a cheesecloth in the bottom of the bamboo steamer.

Add the rice to the cheesecloth and cover the top of the rice with the ends of the cheesecloth. Cover the rice with a lid.

Bring the water to a boil and let the rice steam for 30 minutes or until tender. The rice will be translucent when done. It should stick together and no longer look milky.

For an excellent variation on sticky rice that doesn't require a sticky rice steamer, see Leela Punyaratabandhu's instructions on SheSimmers: http://shesimmers. com/2012/08/how-to-cook-sticky-rice-the-easy-way-and-without-a-steamer.html

Cauliflower Rice

Steamed rice is served with almost everything in Thailand, so substituting cauliflower rice seemed to be the best way to keep up with this tradition while staying Paleo-friendly. Stir-frying the cauliflower causes it to lose some of its pungent flavor, and this method of preparation is actually faster than preparing real rice.

Prep time: 10 minutes
Cook time: 3 to 4 minutes

1/2 cup cauliflower florets per person

1 to 2 tablespoons coconut oil, palm oil, or leaf lard

Place the cauliflower florets in a food processor and process until the pieces are very small, the size of grains of rice.

Heat the oil in a wok over medium-high heat. Once the oil is hot, add the cauliflower.

Stir-fry the cauliflower rice for about 3 to 4 minutes. Serve with any dish in this book that can be served with rice.

Garlic-Infused Vinegar

This common ingredient, which is used in several of the recipes in this book, will add that extra zing to your Thai dishes. Easy to make and fun to use, garlic-infused vinegar is a must-have addition to the Thai condiments that soon will be lining the shelves of your refrigerator. I make mine with coconut vinegar or rice vinegar and love the results.

Gratiam Nam Sohm

Prep time: 20 minutes
Yield: 2 cups

8 to 10 garlic cloves, smashed with the flat side of a knife and halved

2 cups coconut vinegar, white vinegar, or rice vinegar

Add the garlic to a sterilized glass jar.

Heat the vinegar in a small saucepan over medium-high heat until very hot but not yet boiling.

Pour the vinegar over the garlic and close with an airtight lid.

Let the vinegar sit in the refrigerator for at least 2 weeks, gently shaking or stirring every couple of days.

Strain the infused vinegar, discarding the garlic cloves, and store in an airtight jar at room temperature.

Use within 2 months.

You can use this technique to infuse vinegar with almost any herbs or spices, such as rosemary, chiles and cilantro, or even citrus! Get creative and use your infused vinegar to make marinades, sauces, or salad dressings.

Tamarind Paste

Tamarind paste provides the important sour element found in many Thai dishes. The preparation is worth the authentic flavor this special ingredient gives many of the recipes in this book. Tamarind paste can be stored in the refrigerator for up to 2 weeks, or you can freeze it in ice cube trays and store in the freezer in a Ziploc bag for up to 1 year and use as needed.

Makham Piek

Prep time: 10 minutes
Yield: About 2 cups

8 ounces tamarind pods, shelled
2 cups hot water

Place the tamarind in a small bowl.

Pour the hot water over the tamarind and let it sit for 15 to 20 minutes.

Squeeze and massage the tamarind with your fingers until you create a pulp. Remove the seeds and tough membrane by pushing the pulp through a strainer, cheesecloth, or nut milk bag, leaving behind only the tamarind paste.

Toasted Rice Powder

Khao Koor

This is an important ingredient that adds a wonderful aroma and depth of flavor to several Thai recipes. Ninja, the chef at Enjoy Bistro in Bangkok, taught me how to make the authentic version using toasted white sticky rice, lemongrass, and kaffir lime leaves, and I was able replicate the taste and texture by substituting coconut flakes for the rice. If white rice is part of your diet, I have also included directions to make this the authentic way.

Prep time: 10 minutes

Cook time: 3 to 5 minutes if using coconut flakes, 7 to 10 minutes if using raw rice

Yield: 2 cups

10 to 15 kaffir lime leaves, stemmed and torn into quarters

2 stalks lemongrass, thinly sliced

2 cups coconut flakes or 1 cup uncooked sticky rice

Add the kaffir lime leaves and lemongrass to a dry skillet or wok over medium heat and cook, stirring constantly, until the leaves start to crisp and the lemongrass starts to brown, about 5 to 7 minutes.

Add the coconut flakes to the leaves and lemongrass and cook, stirring constantly, until the coconut flakes are brown and crispy, about 3 to 5 minutes.

Place the browned coconut flakes, kaffir lime leaves, and lemongrass in a food processor and pulse until powdery. Keep refrigerated up to 3 weeks and use as needed.

If using sticky rice, add the uncooked rice with the kaffir lime leaves and lemongrass in step 1 and cook over medium to medium-high heat, stirring constantly, until the rice is browned, about 7 to 10 minutes. Then pulse the rice mixture in a food processor or pound in a granite mortar and pestle until finely ground. You can store the rice powder in an airtight container, unrefrigerated, for several months.

Beef Marinade

Use this marinade for the Spicy Grilled Beef Salad (page 106) or any other meat of your choice. You can also use it for a tasty snack: marinate pork or beef, grill, thinly slice, and serve with Nam Jim Jaew (Dried Chili Dipping Sauce, page 66).

Prep time: 10 minutes

Yield: 1/4 cup

1/2 teaspoon ground coriander

1 coriander root, chopped, or 1
   tablespoon chopped cilantro stems

2 cloves garlic

1/2 teaspoon black pepper

1 tablespoon coconut aminos

1 tablespoon Oyster Sauce (page 58)

Using a granite mortar and pestle, pound and mash together the ground coriander, coriander root, and garlic.

Transfer the coriander mixture to a small bowl and stir in the black pepper, coconut aminos, and oyster sauce.

Store in an airtight container in the refrigerator for up to 1 week, or use immediately for Spicy Grilled Beef Salad (page 106).

Chile Oil

This is a staple condiment found on all Thai tables and street carts and in every Thai restaurant. Making it yourself ensures it's made with quality oil and without any unknown fillers, preservatives, or MSG. The best part? It's easy, fresh, and far tastier than the bottled varieties.

Nam Prik

Yield: 1/2 cup

1/2 cup avocado oil

10 small red Thai chiles, thinly sliced (about 1/2 ounce)

Heat the oil in a small sauté pan or skillet over medium-high heat until nice and hot.

Add the chiles to the hot oil and sauté for about 30 seconds, then turn the heat down to low and let the chiles simmer for about 10 minutes, stirring often.

Store the chiles and the oil together in the fridge in a glass jar for up to 3 weeks.

Deep-Fried Garlic

Deep-fried garlic is used as a condiment for soups and stir-frys in Thai cooking and adds a rich, nutty flavor. You will love how great your house smells after making it, and you'll love even more the way it provides an intense and delicious burst of flavor in dishes like Garlic Fried Rice (page 118).

Gratiam Jiaow

Prep time: 10 minutes

Yield: About 1/2 cup

1 bulb garlic or Thai garlic, peeled and finely minced (if using Thai garlic, no need to peel each clove)

1/4 cup palm shortening or leaf lard

Add the garlic and shortening to a cold pan over medium heat. Cook, stirring often, until the minced garlic is golden brown and crispy, about 3 to 5 minutes.

Strain the cooked garlic through a sieve and reserve the oil.

Store both the deep-fried garlic and the garlic oil in airtight containers in the refrigerator for later use. Use the oil within 3 to 4 days and the garlic within 1 week.

Curry Pastes

Making curry paste is an art, a passion, and a sign of a true love for food, spice, and flavor. Although it can be a lot of work, there is something therapeutic and almost Zen-like about combining the intense flavors of galangal, lemongrass, chiles, and spices; hearing the sound of the granite mortar and pestle; and tasting the smooth deliciousness that turns ordinary coconut milk into magic. Yes, you can buy amazing pre-made curries, but please attempt to make your own paste for at least one or two recipes in this book. You will not regret it.

I highly recommend using a granite mortar and pestle to make curry pastes. The granite keeps the ingredients cool and helps preserve their flavor; it also breaks up fibers, almost like cutting or mincing them, which helps to keep the flavors intact. A food processor, in contrast, actually oxidizes some of the ingredients as they get warm, which affects the flavor. However, do not let this deter you from making your own paste if you don't have a mortar and pestle. Homemade is always best, even if you go the food processor route.

To store your curry paste, place it into a glass container and add a teaspoon of avocado oil on top to create an oil layer that helps preserve the paste. It will keep in the refrigerator for up to a month. You can also freeze curry paste for up to 3 months. I recommend freezing it in ice cube trays and then transferring the cubes of paste to plastic freezer bags for storage.

Krung Gaeng

Mortar and Pestle Directions for All Pastes

If the recipe calls for dried chiles, cover them with hot water and let them soak for at least 10 minutes. Remove the seeds, and stem and thoroughly dry the chiles.

If the recipe calls for roasted ingredients, dry roast them in a wok or skillet over medium to medium-low heat, stirring often. Roast spices until they begin to make a popping sound and are fragrant. Roast garlic, shallots, lemongrass, ginger, and galangal separate from the spices until browned and aromatic.

Add the hard dry spices to the mortar first and grind to a powder. Add the salt and chiles next. The salt helps with the grinding process; I recommend using rock salt. For the most effective way to make the paste, place the ingredients as far to one side of the bottom of the mortar as possible, not directly in the center of the bottom, then pound and push the ingredients down into the center with the pestle. Drag them back up the side and pound again, pushing them back to the center, and repeat. You can do this quickly, pounding fast, once you get accustomed to the technique. If you pound straight down in the center onto the ingredients, they can bounce back up at you and get in your eyes, so be careful!

After the dry spices, salt, and chiles are pounded into a paste, add the remaining ingredients except the shrimp paste and continue grinding. This could take up to 20 minutes. It's important to make sure all the fibers are broken down and the ingredients are unrecognizable—you should have a true paste.

Add the shrimp paste and mix and pound it together with the curry paste.

Food Processer
Directions for All Pastes

If the recipe calls for dried chiles, cover them with hot water and let them soak for at least 10 minutes. Remove the seeds, and stem and thoroughly dry the chiles.

If the recipe calls for roasted ingredients, dry roast them in a wok or skillet over medium to medium-low heat, stirring often. Roast spices until they begin to a make a popping sound and are fragrant. Roast garlic, shallots, lemongrass, ginger, and galangal separate from the spices until browned and aromatic.

Add all the ingredients except the shrimp paste to a food processor, Vitamix, or blender. Pulse or blend until smooth. You may need to add a little water to the paste to help with the blending process. Once the mixture is smooth, add the shrimp paste and pulse until blended. Store exactly as recommended for the mortar and pestle preparation.

Yellow Curry Paste

5 large dried red chiles

2 tablespoons thinly sliced lemongrass, tough outer layer removed, roasted

2 tablespoons thinly sliced shallots, roasted

3 tablespoons thinly sliced garlic, roasted

1/2 teaspoon thinly sliced ginger, roasted

1 teaspoon thinly sliced galangal, roasted

1/2 teaspoon coriander seeds, roasted

1/2 teaspoon cumin seeds, roasted

1 tablespoon chopped coriander root or 10 cilantro stems

1/2 teaspoon sea salt

1 1/2 teaspoons curry powder

1 teaspoon fresh turmeric

1 teaspoon shrimp paste

Green Curry Paste

15 medium green Thai chiles, chopped

4 small green Thai chiles, chopped

4 small red Thai chiles, chopped

2 tablespoons thinly sliced lemongrass, tough outer layer removed

1 1/2 teaspoons thinly sliced galangal

1 teaspoon chopped kaffir lime rind

2 tablespoons thinly sliced shallots

2 tablespoons finely chopped garlic

2 tablespoons chopped coriander root or 10 cilantro stems

1 teaspoon fresh turmeric

1/2 teaspoon coriander seeds

1/2 teaspoon cumin seeds

1/4 teaspoon black pepper

1 teaspoon shrimp paste

Red Curry Paste

10 large dried red chiles

4 small red Thai chiles

1/2 teaspoon coriander seeds, roasted

1/4 teaspoon cumin seeds, roasted

1/4 teaspoon black peppercorns, roasted

2 tablespoons thinly sliced lemongrass, tough outer layer removed

1 teaspoon thinly sliced galangal

1 teaspoon coarsely chopped kaffir lime rind

2 tablespoons thinly sliced shallots

3 tablespoons thinly sliced garlic

1 tablespoon chopped coriander root, or 10 cilantro stems, chopped

1 teaspoon shrimp paste

Variations: For Panaeng Curry Paste, add 3 tablespoons of ground and roasted cashews. For Khao Soi Curry Paste, add 1 teaspoon of curry powder.

Massaman Curry Paste

5 large dried red chiles

3 tablespoons thinly sliced garlic, roasted

2 tablespoons thinly sliced shallots, roasted

1 teaspoon thinly sliced galangal, roasted

1 teaspoon finely chopped kaffir lime rind, roasted

1 teaspoon coriander seeds, roasted

1/2 teaspoon cumin seeds, roasted

1 teaspoon black peppercorns, roasted

2 cloves, roasted

2 tablespoons thinly sliced lemongrass, tough outer layer removed

1 tablespoon chopped coriander root or 10 cilantro stems, chopped

1 teaspoon sea salt

1 teaspoon shrimp paste

Southern Sour Curry Paste

6 medium dried red Thai chiles

5 small red Thai chiles

3 cloves garlic

1/4 cup chopped shallots

1 teaspoon shrimp paste

1 (1-inch) piece fresh turmeric, peeled

Pinch of sea salt

Oyster Sauce

Oyster sauce is very common in Thai cooking and, as mentioned in the introduction to the recipe section, finding a decent pre-made oyster sauce that is gluten free and not filled with unnecessary ingredients is very hard to do. I was so happy that this homemade version turned out to be as good as I hoped it would be, because the flavor that oyster sauce imparts in Thai cuisine is extremely important and delicious!

Nam Mun Hoy

Prep time: 10 minutes
Cook time: 20 minutes
Yield: 1/2 cup

1 (8- to 10-ounce) jar of fresh oysters, with liquid

1 tablespoon water

1 teaspoon sea salt

3 tablespoons coconut aminos

2 tablespoons maple syrup

Drain the oysters and reserve the liquid.

Mince the oysters and add them to a small saucepan along with the water and reserved liquid.

Bring to a boil, cover, and let simmer for 10 minutes.

Remove from heat, add the salt, mix well, and let the mixture cool completely.

Once cooled, push the mixture through a sieve into a saucepan.

Add the coconut aminos and maple syrup to the mixture. Simmer for about 10 minutes.

This sauce will not be thick, like the store-bought sauce, but it will add the correct flavor to the recipes in this book that require oyster sauce.

Store in the refrigerator for up to 3 weeks.

Sweet and Sour Sauce

This sauce is used in Pad Priew Wan (Sweet and Sour Stir-Fry, page 176). It also goes well with Pa Pia Sod (Spring Rolls, page 76)—or any other dish in this book that requires a delicious dip!

Nam Jim Priao Wan

Prep time: 10 minutes

Yield: 1/4 cup

2 teaspoons coconut aminos

2 teaspoons raw organic honey

1/4 teaspoon black pepper

1 tablespoon coconut vinegar or rice vinegar

2 tablespoons tomato paste

1 1/2 teaspoons Thai Chili Paste (page 64)

Whisk together all of the ingredients and use as needed.

Store in a glass container in the refrigerator for up to 1 week.

Fish Sauce with Chiles

Nam Pla Prik

I can't imagine eating Thai food without this staple condiment, which is always found on every Thai table. It makes everything taste amazing, and the recipe is so simple it can hardly be called a recipe. There is no right or wrong way to make nam pla prik, and no exact measurements are required. The only requirement is that you always have some on hand!

Prep time: 5 minutes

Small red and green Thai chiles
Fish sauce
Squeeze of lime

Cut several small chiles into small round pieces. I usually use 30 to 40 whole chiles.

Place the sliced chiles into a glass container or bowl and add enough fish sauce to cover them.

Add a squeeze of lime, stir, and store in the refrigerator for up to 2 months (but you'll probably finish it long before then).

Thai Chili Paste

Nam Prik Pao

This staple Thai condiment can be added to any dish in this book. Keep it in the fridge for months, and make sure it is on your table during any Thai feast for those who crave the smoky, spicy, and sweet flavor that is authentic Thai chili paste! Most store-bought versions use soybean oil and sometimes MSG, so it's best to make your own.

Prep time: 30 minutes

Cook time: 40 minutes

Yield: 1 cup

11 to 13 medium red Thai chiles, stemmed

5 cloves garlic, unpeeled

1/2 cup diced white onion

1 tablespoon maple syrup

2 tablespoons water

1 tablespoon coconut vinegar

1/4 teaspoon fish sauce

Preheat oven to 400°F. Set aside two whole chiles.

Spread the garlic, the rest of the chiles, and the onion evenly on a baking sheet and roast, turning occasionally, for 20 to 30 minutes, or until the chiles start to turn black and the garlic and onions are browned and soft.

Remove the baking sheet from the oven and let the roasted veggies cool. When it's cool enough to handle, squeeze the roasted garlic from the peel.

Place the roasted garlic, chiles, onions, two remaining unroasted chiles, maple syrup, water, vinegar, and fish sauce in a food processor or blender and process until finely chopped and well blended.

Add the contents of the food processor to a small saucepan and bring to a simmer over medium-high heat. Turn the heat down to low and simmer for another 5 to 7 minutes.

Store the paste in a glass jar in the refrigerator for up to 2 weeks and use as needed.

Dried Chili Dipping Sauce

Nam Jim Jaew

Nam jim jaew is similar to salsa, but of course totally Thai! I first ate this in Chiang Mai at a beautiful little resort we visited called Baan Pong. Nam jim jaew is traditionally served with thinly sliced cooked pork, and I could have eaten it with a spoon—it was really that good. Eat it with grilled beef that has been prepared with the marinade on page 48, seafood, or Grilled Pork or Chicken (page 84).

Prep time: 10 minutes

Yield: 1/2 cup

2 tablespoons Tamarind Paste (page 44)

2 tablespoons fish sauce

1 teaspoon maple syrup

1 tablespoon dried chili flakes

1 tablespoon minced red onion

1 tablespoon finely chopped sawtooth coriander or cilantro

1/2 teaspoon Khao Koor (Toasted Rice Powder, page 46)

In a small bowl, stir together the tamarind paste, fish sauce, and maple syrup.

Add the chili flakes to the tamarind mixture and combine well.

Add the onion, sawtooth coriander, and rice powder and mix.

Serve immediately or store in the refrigerator for up to 1 week.

"Peanut" Sauce

To accompany the best-ever Chicken Satay (page 82), this is by far the best-ever peanut sauce. I've substituted cashews or almonds for the peanuts, and the results are just as outstanding, if not even better. This recipe is adapted from the original that was taught to me by the amazing Pom of Cooking@home Thai Culinary School in Chiang Mai.

Nam Jim Satay

Prep time: 10 minutes

Cook time: 10 minutes

Yield: 1 1/2 cups

1/2 to 1 cup roasted cashews or almonds

1 cup Coconut Milk (page 32)

1/2 to 1 tablespoon Red Curry Paste (page 55)

2 teaspoons Tamarind Paste (page 44)

1 to 2 teaspoons fish sauce

2 to 3 teaspoons maple syrup or raw organic honey

1/4 teaspoon salt

Using a wooden mortar and pestle, pound the cashews or almonds until finely ground. (You can also use a food processor.)

In a small saucepan, heat the coconut milk over medium-high heat until the fat starts to separate and the coconut milk is simmering, about 2 to 3 minutes.

Add ½ tablespoon of the red curry paste to the coconut milk and whisk together.

Stir half of the ground nuts into the red curry mixture and simmer until the sauce reduces and starts to thicken, about 5 to 7 minutes.

Add the fish sauce, maple syrup, and salt to taste.

If you want the sauce to be spicier, add another ½ tablespoon of the red curry paste. If you want a thicker consistency, add more of the ground nuts until you reach your desired thickness.

Cucumber Relish

ajad

Cucumber relish is traditionally served with Chicken Satay (page 82), but it can add flavor and color to any dish. This is another recipe I learned while studying with Pom at her Cooking@home Thai Culinary School and has been only slightly modified to use maple syrup instead of palm sugar.

Prep time: 10 minutes

Yield: 1 1/2 cups

1/4 cup coconut vinegar or rice vinegar

1/4 teaspoon salt

2 teaspoons maple syrup

1/2 cup sliced cucumber

1/4 cup thinly sliced red onion or shallot

1/4 cup thinly sliced medium red Thai chiles

In a small bowl, mix together the vinegar, salt, and maple syrup.

Add the sliced veggies to the vinegar mixture, toss together, and serve.

Sweet Chili Sauce

Nam Chim Kai

This is such a great condiment to make yourself, thereby avoiding unnecessary fillers, tons of sugar, and thickeners like wheat flour or cornstarch. It's also easy to make and stores well in the refrigerator for up to 2 weeks. The Thai name for this sauce translates to a sauce for chicken, but feel free to use this delicious recipe to add flavor to any dish in this book.

Prep time: 20 minutes
Cook time: 20 to 30 minutes
Yield: About 1 cup

2 medium red Thai chiles, sliced

2 cloves garlic

1/2 cup coconut vinegar or rice vinegar

1/4 cup raw organic honey

1/2 cup water

1/2 cup pineapple juice

1 teaspoon sea salt

Using a wooden mortar and pestle, pound the chiles and garlic into a paste.

In a small saucepan, combine the chile and garlic mixture, vinegar, honey, water, pineapple juice, and salt, and bring to a simmer.

Simmer, stirring occasionally, for about 20 to 30 minutes, or until the sauce thickens.

Remove from heat and serve with Deep-Fried Fish Cakes (page 202), Grilled Pork or Chicken (page 84), or other dishes of your choice.

Appetizers and Salads

Spring Rolls	76
Leaf Bites	78
Garlic-Fried Prawns	80
Chicken Satay	82
Grilled Pork or Chicken	84
Deep-Fried Chicken with Creamy Lime Sauce	86
Northern-Style Chili	88
Pork Rinds	90
Papaya Salad	92
Pomelo Salad	94
Spicy Cucumber Salad	96
Thai Seafood or Ground Meat Salad	98
Pork Salad with Spicy Lime Dressing	100
Spicy Snow Mushroom Salad	102
Spicy Mixed Fruit Salad	104
Spicy Grilled Beef Salad	106
Glass Noodle Salad	108
Green Mango Salad	110

Spring Rolls

I opted for napa cabbage leaves instead of the usual rice paper for a traditional Thai spring roll with a twist, but feel free to use the traditional spring roll rice paper if you like. Serve these with Sweet Chili Sauce (page 72) for an awesome appetizer or snack.

Pa Pia Sod

Prep time: 30 minutes

Cook time: 10 minutes

Serves: 3 to 5

6 to 8 large napa cabbage leaves

1 tablespoon coconut oil, palm oil, or leaf lard

3 cloves garlic, minced

1 cup ground pork, chicken, or beef

1/4 cup finely grated carrots

1/2 cup finely shredded cabbage

1/2 cup finely sliced shiitake mushrooms

1 teaspoon coconut aminos

1 teaspoon fish sauce

1 teaspoon Oyster Sauce (page 58)

1/4 teaspoon black pepper

Bring a large pot of water to a boil and blanch the cabbage leaves to make them easy to fold. Drain and thoroughly dry the leaves and set aside to cool.

Heat the oil in a wok over medium-high heat, add the garlic, and stir-fry until fragrant, about 30 seconds.

Brown the meat in the oil and garlic.

Add the carrots, shredded cabbage, and mushrooms to the meat and stir-fry for 2 to 3 minutes.

Add the coconut aminos, fish sauce, oyster sauce, and black pepper to the meat and vegetable mixture.

Spoon 1 to 2 tablespoons of the mixture into the middle of each cabbage leaf.

Cut off the thick white stem at the bottom of the leaf, fold each side of the leaf over the filling, and roll until the stuffing is concealed.

Cut the rolls in half and serve.

Leaf Bites

Miang Kham

This is a surprisingly scrumptious appetizer and tons of fun for gatherings with friends and family. Traditionally, it uses leaves of the pak miang, a plant grown in Southeast Asia whose large leaves are somewhat reminiscent of spinach leaves. Our kids love to create their own versions of Leaf Bites, and I hope you also feel inspired to change the ingredients based on your own particular tastes. As the result of the fun we have had making Leaf Bites, these are now a staple snack in our kitchen, with or without a special occasion!

Prep time: 20 minutes

Finely shredded coconut

Dried shrimp

Shallots or red onion, finely diced

Lime, finely chopped, with rind

Ginger, minced

Small red Thai chiles, chopped

Cashews, roasted and coarsely chopped

Large pak miang or spinach leaves

Nam Jim Jaew (Dried Chili Dipping Sauce, page 66), Sweet Chili Sauce (page 72), or Nam Pla Prik (Fish Sauce with Chiles, page 62), to serve

On a serving platter, place small piles of each ingredient.

Let everyone serve themselves by filling the center of a leaf with ingredients of their choice and a little bit of sauce, and wrapping it up.

Garlic-Fried Prawns

Goong Tod Kratiem Prik Thai

I'm fairly confident that I ate my own weight in garlic-fried prawns while visiting Enjoy Bistro in Bangkok. Once I started making it myself at home, it became painfully clear that you must pound the garlic with a mortar and pestle, or at least smash the cloves with the flat part of your knife and then slice them. Smashed garlic cooks at the same rate as the prawns and will not burn, but using minced garlic results in burnt garlic and a mess. Cook with care—this dish can splatter while frying, so use a splatter guard. Special thanks to Ninja, the chef I cooked with at Enjoy Bistro during our stay in Bangkok, for teaching me this amazing recipe.

Prep time: 20 minutes

Cook time: 4 to 5 minutes

Serves: 2 to 3

10 cloves garlic

8 to 10 medium prawns, shelled and deveined

1/2 teaspoon sea salt

1 tablespoon Oyster Sauce (page 58)

1 tablespoon fish sauce

1 cup palm shortening or leaf lard

Cilantro, for garnish

Lime wedges, to serve

Cucumber slices, to serve

Sweet Chili Sauce (page 72), to serve

Use a wooden mortar and pestle to crush the garlic, or smash it with the flat side of a knife and then slice.

In a small bowl, combine the garlic, prawns, sea salt, oyster sauce, and fish sauce. Mix together until the prawns are coated.

Heat the shortening in a wok over high heat until very hot (the prawns should sizzle as soon as they hit the oil).

Turn the heat down to medium-high and add the prawns immediately.

Cook the prawns in the hot oil, stirring gently, for 4 to 5 minutes.

Remove the prawns from the wok with a metal strainer. Serve with cilantro, lime, cucumber slices, and Sweet Chili Sauce (page 72).

Chicken Satay

The key to this delicious chicken satay is grilling the chicken and basting it often with the sauce. The basting ensures that none of the flavor is lost during the cooking process and helps to lock in the natural juices of the chicken so that the end result is tender and flavorful. Grilling small pieces of chicken can be challenging, so be sure to not overcook these and turn them often while keeping them coated with the wonderful marinade. Special thanks to Pom from the Cooking@home Thai Culinary School for this recipe—it is truly the best chicken satay I have ever eaten.

Satay Gai

Prep time: 30 minutes + at least 30 minutes to marinate

Cook time: 5 to 10 minutes

Serves: 2 to 3

2 chicken breasts

Marinade

1 tablespoon thinly sliced lemongrass

1 tablespoon finely chopped galangal

1 tablespoon Oyster Sauce (page 58)

1 tablespoon coconut aminos

2 teaspoons raw organic honey

1 tablespoon melted butter, coconut oil, or ghee

1 teaspoon avocado oil or extra virgin olive oil

1/2 teaspoon yellow curry

1 teaspoon ground coriander

1/2 teaspoon ground cumin

2 tablespoons Coconut Milk (page 32)

Nam Jim Satay ("Peanut" Sauce, page 68), to serve

Ajad (Cucumber Relish, page 70), to serve

Cut the chicken breasts into pieces about 3 to 4 inches long, 1 inch wide, and 1/4 inch thick.

Using a granite mortar and pestle, pound together the lemongrass and galangal to make a paste.

In a medium bowl, combine the lemongrass and galangal paste with the remaining marinade ingredients.

Place half the marinade in a plastic bag and reserve the rest for basting the chicken. Add the chicken pieces to the plastic bag and coat thoroughly with the marinade.

Let the chicken marinate in the refrigerator for at least 30 minutes.

Thread the marinated chicken pieces onto wooden skewers and grill over high heat for about 5 to 7 minutes, or until the juices run clear, turning often and basting frequently with the reserved marinade.

Serve with Nam Jim Satay ("Peanut" Sauce, page 68) and Ajad (Cucumber Relish, page 70).

Grilled Pork or Chicken

Although known as common street food, this recipe is not at all ordinary when it comes to flavor! The secret to this amazing yet simple dish is to marinate the meat overnight in coconut milk. I'm confident that your family will love it just as much as mine.

Moo Ping / Kai Yang

Prep time: 20 minutes + overnight to marinate

Cook time: 4 to 6 minutes

Serves: 2 to 3

1/2 pound pork loin or pork chops or 2 chicken breasts

1 cup Coconut Milk (page 32)

1 tablespoon black pepper

1 teaspoon salt

1/2 teaspoon whole cane sugar (optional)

1 tablespoon coconut oil

Napa cabbage, shredded, for garnish

Sliced cucumber, for garnish

Cilantro, for garnish

Sweet Chili Sauce (page 72) or Nam Jim Jaew (Dried Chili Dipping Sauce, page 66), to serve

Cut the pork or chicken into pieces about 4 inches long and 1/4 inch thick.

Marinate the pork or chicken overnight in the coconut milk.

Combine the black pepper, salt, and whole cane sugar and set aside.

Remove the meat from the coconut milk, brushing off the excess. Sprinkle the spice mixture on both sides of the pieces of meat.

Heat the coconut oil in a skillet over medium-high heat.

Sear the meat on both sides, about a minute or two per side.

Garnish with shredded napa cabbage, cucumber slices, and cilantro, and serve with Sweet Chili Sauce (page 72).

Deep-Fried Chicken with Creamy Lime Sauce

Dai Drob Ma Nao

We were introduced to this dish while staying at Baan Pong in Chiang Mai, and it reminds me of a kind of Thai pub fare. Although it's usually made with wheat flour, I use my version of tempura batter and make the sauce with homemade mayonnaise. My kids can't get enough of this dish, and it's super fun to make—great party food for your Thai-inspired get-together. Make sure the kale leaves are completely dry before you deep-fry them so you don't end up with soggy, burnt, oil-spattering kale instead of crispy, crunchy kale goodness.

Prep time: 30 to 45 minutes

Cook time: 7 to 10 minutes

Serves: 3 to 4

Creamy Lime Sauce

3 tablespoons homemade mayo (recipe found online at www.everydaypaleo.com)

1 tablespoon fresh lime juice

1 tablespoon raw organic honey or maple syrup

1 bunch kale

Tempura Batter

1/2 cup tapioca flour

2 tablespoons sparkling water

1 egg

Pinch of sea salt

1 to 2 cups palm shortening or leaf lard

1 chicken breast, cut into 2-inch cubes

Whisk together the sauce ingredients and set aside.

Wash and thoroughly dry the kale and remove the leaves from the tough stem.

Cut the kale into very thin strips and set aside.

Whisk together the tempura batter ingredients in a medium bowl and set aside.

Heat the shortening in a wok over high heat.

Once the shortening is completely melted and very hot, add the kale strips and cook for about 30 seconds, or until just crispy, stirring constantly. Watch the kale closely because it can quickly go from perfect to burnt.

Remove the kale from the hot oil with a slotted spoon and set aside to drain.

Coat the chicken pieces in the prepared batter.

Gently drop the battered chicken into the already-hot oil and deep-fry, turning often, until golden brown, about 4 to 5 minutes.

Remove the chicken from the hot oil and place on top of the crispy kale.

Serve immediately with the lime sauce.

Northern-Style Chili

Nam Prik Ong

I was blown away when I ate this dish at the Baan Pong resort in Chiang Mai. I felt as if I were eating the classic American favorite of good ol' chili and corn chips, but with distinct Thai flavors and ingredients—ground pork instead of beef and deep-fried pork rinds instead of corn chips. It's a wonderful Thai party food and makes for a crowd-pleasing appetizer that your friends and family can enjoy as you prep for your Thai dinner party!

Prep time: 10 minutes

Cook time: 15 minutes

Serves: 2 to 3

1 tablespoon Thai Chili Paste (page 64)

1 tablespoon tomato paste

1 tablespoon minced red onion

3 cloves garlic

1 small red Thai chile

1/2 pound ground pork

1 cup diced tomatoes

1/4 cup chicken broth

1 teaspoon maple syrup

Sea salt

Using a wooden mortar and pestle, mash together the chili paste, tomato paste, red onion, garlic, and small red Thai chile.

Heat the chile mixture in a wok over medium-high to high heat and add the ground pork. Mix together well and cook for 4 to 5 minutes.

Add the tomatoes, chicken broth, and maple syrup to the pork mixture.

Simmer, stirring occasionally, until the sauce thickens, approximately 10 minutes.

Season with sea salt to taste and serve with Cap Moo (Pork Rinds, page 90).

Pork Rinds

Cap Moo

I remember watching these get made by the gallon, literally, in an amazing market in Chiang Mai. I walked around a corner and saw a man pulling huge amounts of pork skin strips out of a giant cauldron of hot oil. The smell of puffed and fried pork skin filled the air, and I couldn't wait to sink my teeth into this northern Thai staple. These are especially good with Nam Prik Ong (Northern-Style Chili, page 88). I must take a moment to thank my friend and volunteer guide to Chiang Mai, Mark Ritchie, for taking us to the market and for enhancing our trip greatly with his knowledge and kindness.

Prep time: 45 minutes

Cook time: 10 minutes

3 tablespoons salt

8 cups water

1/2 pound pork skin with fat, cut into pieces that are 1 inch wide and 2 inches long (about 3 cups)

2 cups palm shortening or leaf lard

Preheat the oven to 250°F.

Add the salt to the water and bring to a boil.

Drop the pork rinds into the boiling water and cook for 5 minutes.

Drain the rinds and pat dry.

Spread the rinds evenly on a baking sheet and place in the pre-heated oven.

Let the pork rinds dry in the oven for approximately 30 minutes, but watch them carefully and remove them immediately once they appear shiny and dry.

Heat the shortening in a large wok over high heat.

Once the oil is hot enough to sizzle when you place one end of a pork rind into it, fry in small batches until the pork rinds puff up, typically about 7 to 10 minutes.

Drain and serve.

Papaya Salad

The sound of the wooden mortar and pestle; the smell of fresh lime, garlic, and chiles; the feel of the grater hitting the green papaya—every time I make this dish I am magically transported back to Thailand. We ate som tum in every region we visited in Thailand, but the best version I found was when we were in Bangkok cooking with Nusi at his Silom Thai Cooking School, and that's the recipe I've included here. I know you will enjoy its freshness and flavor just as much as I do.

Som Tum

Prep time: 30 minutes

Serves: 3 to 4

3 tablespoons cashews

4 to 5 cloves garlic

1 to 2 small red Thai chiles, diced

2 tablespoons dried shrimp

1 cup diced long beans or green beans

5 to 6 cherry tomatoes, halved

2 tablespoons fish sauce

1 tablespoon maple syrup

Juice from 1 lime (about 1 1/2 tablespoons)

1 tablespoon Tamarind Paste (page 44)

2 cups shredded green papaya

1/2 cup shredded carrots

First, roast the cashews in a dry skillet or wok over medium-high heat, stirring constantly, until the cashews turn a golden brown, about 3 to 5 minutes. Remove from heat immediately and set aside.

Using a wooden mortar and pestle, combine the garlic, chiles, and cashews and pound until they begin to make a paste.

Add the shrimp, long beans, and tomatoes to the mortar. Alternate gently mashing with the pestle and stirring with a spoon to release the tomatoes' juices.

Add the fish sauce, maple syrup, lime juice, and tamarind paste, and stir.

Add the green papaya and shredded carrots and gently stir.

Serve immediately.

Pomelo Salad

My first taste of yam som-o was at the amazing Ginger Kafe restaurant in Chiang Mai. My friend Mark Ritchie recommended this establishment, and I'm so glad that he did. Pomelo salad is a special dish in Thailand. It can't be bought from food carts; it's made in homes for special occasions, or you can find it in fancier restaurants. The crisp sourness of the pomelo mixed with the sweetness of the prawns and the bite of the onion is simply perfect.

Yam Som-O

Prep time: 35 minutes

Cook time: 2 to 3 minutes

Serves: 2 to 3

2 teaspoons fish sauce

2 teaspoons maple syrup

1/2 tablespoon Tamarind Paste (page 44)

1 teaspoon Thai Chili Paste (page 64)

1/2 cup palm shortening or leaf lard

1 tablespoon thinly sliced red onion or shallot

1 tablespoon finely shredded coconut

1 clove garlic, minced

1/4 cup cashews, chopped

6 small shrimp, shelled and deveined

1 cup pomelo or grapefruit, peeled and finely chopped

Mint leaves, for garnish

In a small bowl, combine the fish sauce, maple syrup, tamarind paste, and chili paste, and set aside.

Heat the palm shortening in a small saucepan over medium-high heat.

Once the oil sizzles when an onion piece is dropped in, brown the onion, coconut, and garlic, stirring constantly to avoid burning. Remove from oil and set aside.

In a small, dry sauté pan, add the cashews and turn the heat to medium-high. Stirring or shaking the pan constantly, roast the cashews until golden brown, about 3 to 5 minutes. Remove from the pan and set aside.

Bring a small pot of water to boil. Drop in the shrimp and boil until they are pink and firm and float to the top. Drain and rinse under cool water and set aside.

In a small bowl, pour the fish sauce and maple syrup mixture over the pomelo and mix well.

Place the cooked shrimp on top of the pomelo and sprinkle with the fried onions, garlic, coconut, and cashews.

Garnish with mint leaves and serve.

Spicy Cucumber Salad

Som Tum Taeng Lao

A cousin to the papaya salad, som tum taeng lao is a great way to prepare cucumbers to accompany any dish in this book. Refreshing, spicy, cool, tangy, and just a little sweet, this dish is quintessential Thai cuisine. If you do not have a mortar and pestle, you can use a food processor instead. Ninja, the chef at Enjoy Bistro in Bangkok, introduced me to this dish, and one of the kitchen staff at Enjoy expertly cut the cucumber by holding and turning it in one hand and quickly slicing it with an extremely sharp knife in the other. This technique was amazing to watch, but it's not one I would recommend trying at home. Thank goodness for julienne cutters and the grate blade on my food processor!

Prep time: 20 minutes

Serves: 2 to 3

3 small Thai red chiles

1 to 2 cloves garlic

1 tablespoon maple syrup

2 tablespoons cashews

2 tablespoons dried shrimp

4 cherry tomatoes

1 tablespoon fish sauce

Juice of 1 lime

1 tablespoon Garlic-Infused Vinegar (page 42)

3 small cucumbers, julienned

Cilantro, for garnish

Using a wooden mortar and pestle, pound together the chiles and garlic until they start to make a paste.

Add the maple syrup, cashews, and shrimp to the chile mixture and continue to mash together until the nuts are broken down.

Add the tomatoes, fish sauce, lime juice, and vinegar to the mixture. Alternate stirring with a spoon and gently mashing with the pestle until the tomatoes are slightly mashed.

Add the cucumber to the mixture and gently stir and mash for another minute, or until the juice from the cucumber is released and mixes with the other ingredients. The cucumber should not be mashed to a pulp; the pestle is used just to gently release some of the juices to help bring all the flavors together. The cucumber should still look grated after you gently mash and stir the ingredients together.

Serve garnished with cilantro.

Thai Seafood or Ground Meat Salad

Larb

This delicious and fresh staple from northeastern Thailand is found in many variations all over the country. It's also referred to as laab. I first tried it at Enjoy Bistro in Bangkok, and the spicy, yummy, tart goodness was a huge hit. Adjust the spiciness and fish sauce to your taste and always serve it with fresh raw veggies.

Prep time: 30 minutes (+ 15 minutes to make Khao Koor, Toasted Rice Powder)

Cook time: 15 minutes

Serves: 2 to 3

1/4 cup chicken broth (omit if using ground pork or beef)

1 tablespoon coconut oil or leaf lard (omit if using prawns)

5 large prawns or 1 cup ground pork or beef

2 green onions, white and green parts, chopped

1/4 cup chopped cilantro

1/2 shallot, sliced lengthwise

5 to 7 kaffir lime leaves, chiffonaded

Juice of 1 lime

2 tablespoons Garlic-Infused Vinegar (page 42)

1 tablespoon fish sauce

3 teaspoons Khao Koor (Toasted Rice Powder, page 46)

1 teaspoon dried red chili flakes

1 tablespoon fresh mint leaves, plus more for garnish

Fresh Thai basil, for garnish

Cucumber slices, for garnish

Long beans or green beans, for garnish

Green cabbage, shredded, for garnish

Seafood

In a small saucepan, bring the chicken broth to a simmer and add the prawns, green onions, cilantro, shallot, and kaffir lime leaves. Poach, stirring frequently, until the shrimp is pink and firm. Drain off the stock and transfer the cooked shrimp, veggies, and herbs to a small mixing bowl.

Add the lime juice, vinegar, fish sauce, rice powder, red chili flakes, and mint leaves to the shrimp mixture and combine well.

Garnish with the basil, cucumber slices, long beans, mint leaves, and shredded green cabbage.

Ground Pork or Beef

In a wok, heat the coconut oil or lard over medium-high heat.

Add the ground pork or beef and cook until the meat is browned.

Remove from heat and immediately add the remaining ingredients. Mix well and serve. Garnish with basil, cucumber slices, long beans, mint leaves, and shredded cabbage.

Pork Salad with Spicy Lime Dressing

Moo Manao

This is a quick and easy salad that's traditionally super spicy, but if you are sensitive to spice, you can also make it with just a little bit of heat. This salad is very fresh, intense, bright, and tasty, which is a great overall description of the recipes created and shared by Ninja at Enjoy Bistro in Bangkok.

Prep time: 30 minutes
Cook time: 4 to 5 minutes
Serves: 2 to 3

1/2 cup water

1/2 pound pork loin, thinly sliced

Pinch of salt

1 teaspoon coconut oil

Dressing

2 to 3 cloves garlic

5 to 10 small red or green Thai chiles

1 coriander root, chopped, or 1/4 cup chopped cilantro stems

2 teaspoons maple syrup

4 tablespoons Garlic-Infused Vinegar (page 42)

2 tablespoons fish sauce

Juice of 2 limes

1 cup shredded green cabbage, to serve

2 cloves garlic, thinly sliced, to serve

Small handful of mint leaves, for garnish

In a small saucepan, heat the water over high heat until it just starts to get warm. Add the pork, salt, and coconut oil.

Bring to a simmer and cook for just a minute or two, until the pork is no longer pink but is still tender.

Remove the pork from the water and set aside.

To make the dressing: Using a granite mortar and pestle, pound the chiles, garlic, and coriander root into a paste. Transfer the paste to a small bowl and mix in the maple syrup, vinegar, fish sauce, and lime juice.

Place the shredded cabbage on a plate and layer on the pork, garlic, and dressing (or serve the dressing on the side). Garnish with fresh mint leaves and serve.

Spicy Snow Mushroom Salad

Yam Hed Hou Nou Khow

The first time we ate this salad, our photographer's wife and my dear friend America and I looked at each other in disbelief at just how good it was! I had never had snow mushrooms (also known as white fungus, the less-pretty name) before coming to Thailand and had no idea what to expect. They are tender and soak up all the goodness of the dressing, and they're perfect for a salad, especially when paired with the crunchy veggies and flavorful pork and shrimp. I could eat this salad every day and not get tired of it—and in fact I did, while staying at the beautiful Baan Pong in Chiang Mai.

Prep time: 30 minutes

Cook time: 5 to 7 minutes

Serves: 3 to 4

1 1/2 ounces dried snow mushrooms

1/4 pound ground pork (about 1/2 cup)

1 teaspoon coconut aminos

1/2 teaspoon black pepper

10 medium shrimp, shelled and deveined

Dressing

3 to 8 small red Thai chiles

1 1/2 tablespoons maple syrup

1 1/2 tablespoons fish sauce

3 to 4 tablespoons lime juice

1/2 cup sliced carrots

1/4 cup thinly sliced shallots

1/2 cup quartered cherry tomatoes

1/4 cup sliced celery

1/4 cup sliced green onions, green and white parts

1/4 cup chopped cilantro

Sea salt

Add enough water to a large soup pot to cover the mushrooms and bring the water to a boil. Drop the dried mushrooms into the boiling water, turn the heat down to medium, and let simmer while you prepare the pork.

In a small bowl, mix together the ground pork, coconut aminos, and black pepper.

Pinch off small meatballs of the pork mixture and add them to the simmering water with the mushrooms.

Add the shrimp to the soup pot and continue to simmer for about 2 minutes, or until the shrimp float and are firm and pink and the mushrooms are soft and have been rehydrated. Drain the contents of the pot, rinse everything quickly with cool water, drain again, and set aside.

Make the dressing: Using a wooden mortar and pestle, mash the chiles. Then, in a small bowl, combine the mashed chiles, maple syrup, fish sauce, and lime juice.

Break the rehydrated mushrooms apart into bite-sized pieces, cutting off the bottom yellow part.

Transfer the mushrooms, pork meatballs, and cooked shrimp to a large bowl and add the carrots, shallots, tomatoes, celery, green onions, and cilantro.

Pour the prepared dressing over the salad, mix well, taste and season with sea salt if needed, and serve.

Spicy Mixed Fruit Salad

Som Tum Pon

I was very surprised by this salad when Chef Jim at Baan Pong first made it for us. I'd always loved som tum made with shredded green papaya and equally enjoyed the cucumber version, but I never imagined fruit, veggies, and spices all melding together so well. Som tum pon is refreshing, exciting, and fun to make, and you can adjust the spiciness to suit your preference.

Prep time: 30 minutes

Serves: 2 to 3

3 to 4 cloves garlic

2 to 5 small red or green Thai chiles

1/2 tablespoon maple syrup

1 1/2 tablespoons lime juice

1 1/2 tablespoons fish sauce

1/4 cup dried shrimp

1/4 cup chopped long beans or green beans, plus more for garnish

1/4 cup shredded carrots

3 to 4 large cherry tomatoes, quartered

1/2 cup diced pineapple

1/2 cup halved grapes

1/2 cup diced apple

1/2 cup diced cantaloupe or ripe papaya

Green cabbage, shredded, for garnish (optional)

Using a wooden mortar and pestle, pound the garlic and chiles to make a paste.

Add the maple syrup, lime juice, and fish sauce to the mortar. Mix together with a spoon and pound with the pestle until smooth and well combined.

Add the dried shrimp, long beans, carrots, and tomatoes to the mortar. Gently press with the pestle and mix with a spoon just until the tomatoes are softened and have released their juices. Add the pineapple, grapes, apple, and cantaloupe to the mixture in the mortar and gently press and mix well with a spoon. The finished product should still be intact and not mashed—gently press with the pestle to release some of the juices from the fruit, but do not literally smash the fruit.

Garnish with more long beans and shredded green cabbage and serve.

Spicy Grilled Beef Salad

Yam Nua Yang

This is one of our favorites! When I made this salad for this first time back at home, with the help of my friend and travel partner America, we practically fell all over ourselves to get to the finished product. I often craved yam nua yang while in Thailand and was always happy to see this dish on a menu—and even happier to learn how to make it under the guidance of Chef Jim while staying at the Baan Pong resort in Chiang Mai.

Prep time: 20 minutes (+ overnight to marinate)

Cook time: 4 to 5 minutes

Serves: 2 to 3

1/2 pound sirloin or flank steak

1/4 cup Beef Marinade (page 48)

1 tablespoon maple syrup

2 teaspoons lime juice

2 tablespoons fish sauce

2 to 6 small red Thai chiles, chopped

1 cup thinly sliced cucumber

1/4 cup sliced red onion or shallots

1 green onion, sliced

1/4 cup celery leaves

1/4 cup mint leaves

Lime wedges, for garnish

1 cup shredded cabbage, to serve

Marinate the steak overnight in the beef marinade.

In a small bowl, stir together the maple syrup, lime juice, fish sauce, and chiles.

To grill the steak, heat the grill to high, shake the excess marinade off of the steak, and place it on the grill. Cook for approximately 4 to 5 minutes per side for medium-rare, 5 to 7 minutes for medium, or 8 to 10 minutes for well done. The steaks should be golden brown and slightly charred. Let rest for at least 10 minutes.

To cook the steak in a skillet, heat a large skillet over medium-high heat for about 1 minute. Once the pan is hot, take the steak out of the marinade and shake off any excess. Place the steak in the skillet and sear for 3 to 5 minutes per side for rare to medium-rare, 5 to 8 minutes for medium to medium-well, or 8 to 10 minutes for well done. For thicker steaks, sear for 3 to 5 minutes per side and then roast in a 400°F oven for 5 to 7 minutes. Let the steak rest for at least 10 minutes.

Once it has rested, thinly slice the cooked beef and add it to the maple syrup mixture. Add in the cucumber, red onion, green onion, celery leaves, and mint leaves, and mix well.

Garnish with lime wedges and serve on a bed of shredded cabbage.

Glass Noodle Salad

Glass noodles are made from mung beans, which are a legume and therefore are usually avoided by folks sticking to a Paleo lifestyle. If you can enjoy legumes now and then without any problems, go ahead and use glass noodles; however, you can easily substitute kelp noodles or, my favorite, finely shredded napa cabbage. Any way that you choose to make this, I can guarantee that the outcome will be good!

Yum Wun Sen

Prep time: 30 minutes

Cook time: 3 to 4 minutes

Serves: 2 to 3

1 tablespoon coconut oil, palm oil, or leaf lard

1/2 boneless skinless chicken breast, finely diced (about 1/2 cup)

1 tablespoon fish sauce, divided

1 1/2 ounces kelp noodles or glass noodles, or 1 cup finely shredded napa or green cabbage

1 green onion, white and green parts, diced

1/2 cup coarsely chopped Chinese celery or regular celery with leaves

1 small tomato, sliced

1 to 2 small red Thai chiles, minced

1/2 small white onion, sliced

1 tablespoon minced garlic

1 tablespoon lime juice

1 teaspoon maple syrup or orange juice

1 tablespoon diced cilantro

3 to 4 large lettuce leaves, to serve

Heat the oil in a wok over medium-high heat. Add the chicken and a dash of the fish sauce and stir-fry for 3 to 4 minutes, or until cooked through.

Prepare the noodles. For kelp noodles, simply rinse them well and then submerge in warm water for 10 minutes to soften. I also suggest cutting kelp noodles to make them easier to eat, as they are quite long. For glass noodles, bring a large pot of water to a boil, add the noodles, and boil for 5 to 7 minutes, then drain and rinse with cold water. If you decide to use cabbage, shred or thinly slice 1 cup of napa or green cabbage.

In a medium mixing bowl, combine the chicken and noodles or cabbage.

Add the green onion, celery, tomato, chiles, white onion, and garlic to the chicken mixture and mix well.

Add the lime juice, remaining scant tablespoon of fish sauce, and maple syrup and toss together.

Add the cilantro, toss gently, and serve on a bed of lettuce.

Green Mango Salad

Som Tum Mamuang

Like its cousin Som Tum (Papaya Salad, page 92), this is a refreshing treat traditionally made with a mortar and pestle. I like to serve it with some of the spicier Thai dishes, such as Gang Hung Ley (Northern-Style Slow-Cooked Pork, page 144) or Pad Prik Kung (Stir-Fried Chili Shrimp, page 186), along with Sticky Rice (page 38) or Cauliflower Rice (page 40). All the flavors combine to make an authentic Thai meal and a truly wonderful experience.

Prep time: 20 minutes
Serves: 2 to 3

1/4 cup dried shrimp

1 to 4 small red Thai chiles

1 to 2 cloves garlic

1 to 2 tablespoons lime juice

1 to 2 tablespoons fish sauce

1 tablespoon maple syrup

1 cup peeled and shredded green mango

1/2 cup shredded carrots

1/4 cup thinly sliced shallots

1/4 cup roasted cashews

Using a wooden mortar and pestle, pound the dried shrimp until it's broken apart into small pieces. Transfer the shrimp to a small bowl and set aside.

Add the chiles and garlic to the mortar and pestle and pound together into a paste.

To the small bowl with the shrimp, add the chile and garlic paste, lime juice, fish sauce, and maple syrup. Mix well.

In a medium mixing bowl, combine the mango, carrots, shallots, and cashews. Pour the contents of the small bowl over the salad and toss together.

Serve immediately.

Fried Rice, Noodles,
and Egg Dishes

Thai Fried Rice

Khaw Pahd

Who doesn't love fried rice? And Thai fried rice is special because it's made with white jasmine rice rather than long grain rice and is usually more substantial, boasting bigger pieces of meat and vegetables. This recipe offers directions for cauliflower rice or jasmine rice (page 36) so you can choose which variation of this recipe fits best into your lifestyle. If you use cauliflower rice, the trick is to sauté the cauliflower long enough to let it soak up the flavors of the dish.

The only way to serve Thai fried rice is with nam pla prik, the classic fish sauce with chiles (page 62). I know you'll enjoy it!

Prep time: 30 minutes

Cook time: 8 to 10 minutes

Serves: 2 to 3

3 tablespoons coconut oil or palm oil, divided

1/2 cup finely diced chicken

2 cloves garlic, minced

1/4 cup finely diced onion

1/4 cup finely diced carrots

1 cup Cauliflower Rice (page 40) or cooked Jasmine Rice (page 36)

1/2 teaspoon maple syrup

1/4 teaspoon black pepper

1/2 teaspoon coconut aminos

1 egg

Sea salt

1 green onion, white and green parts, diced, for garnish

Heat 2 tablespoons of the oil in a wok over medium-high heat.

Add the chicken and stir-fry for about 30 seconds.

Add the garlic, onions, and carrots and stir-fry for another minute.

Add the cauliflower rice or jasmine rice and sauté for 2 minutes. Add the maple syrup, black pepper, and coconut aminos and sauté for another minute.

Push the rice mixture to the side of the wok, add the last tablespoon of oil, and crack the egg into the wok. Break the yolk and scramble the egg as it cooks.

Once the egg starts to firm, combine it with the rice mixture.

Taste and season with sea salt or more coconut aminos if needed.

Garnish with the green onion and serve immediately.

Fried Rice with Pineapple and Prawns

*Khao Pahd Sup
Pa Rod Goong Sod*

I am so grateful to have had the chance to take a cooking class at Cooking@home Thai Culinary School in Chiang Mai with the owner, Pom. I loved watching Pom cook; she always put her own personal touch on authentic Thai dishes. This recipe is a shining example of Pom's creativity and her lively, fun spirit. Not just another "rice" dish, Pom's version of Thai-inspired pineapple fried rice steps it up a notch with a touch of curry powder and a bright squeeze of lime to finish off the dish.

Prep time: 30 minutes

Cook time: 8 to 10 minutes

Serves: 2 to 3

1 1/2 cups Cauliflower Rice (page 40) or cooked Jasmine Rice (page 36)

1/2 teaspoon maple syrup

2 teaspoons coconut aminos

1/2 teaspoon yellow curry powder

1 tablespoon coconut oil, palm oil, or leaf lard

4 large prawns, shelled and deveined

2 eggs, beaten

2 cloves garlic, minced

1/4 cup peeled and diced carrots

1/4 cup finely chopped pineapple

1/4 cup roasted cashews

3 to 4 green onions, diced

Sea salt and black pepper

1 tomato, sliced, for garnish

1 small cucumber, peeled and thinly sliced, for garnish

1 lime, cut into small wedges, for garnish

In a small bowl, mix together the cauliflower rice or jasmine rice, maple syrup, coconut aminos, and yellow curry powder.

In a wok, heat the oil over medium-high heat. Add the prawns and stir-fry for about 1 to 2 minutes, until they turn pink. Push the prawns over to the side of the wok, pour the beaten eggs into the middle of the wok, and cook through.

Add the rice mixture to the wok and then add the garlic, carrots, pineapple, cashews, and green onions. Stir-fry for 4 to 5 minutes.

Push the prawns from the side of the wok back into the rice mixture and stir-fry together for just a few seconds. Add sea salt and black pepper to taste and adjust seasoning as desired.

Garnish with the tomato slices, cucumber slices, and lime wedges, and serve.

Garlic Fried Rice

This is such a treat. When I ate this for the first time in Thailand, it was at restaurant in Kao Lok. I re-created it from memory at home using cauliflower instead of rice, and it's so yummy, I could eat this alone for a meal! You can also, of course, feel free to use jasmine rice instead of cauliflower rice.

Kao Pahd Kra Tiam

Prep time: 30 minutes

Cook time: 8 to 10 minutes

Serves: 2 to 3

3 tablespoons coconut or palm oil, divided

10 to 12 cloves garlic, pounded in a granite mortar and pestle or minced

1 cup Cauliflower Rice (page 40), uncooked, or cooked Jasmine Rice (page 36)

2 eggs

2 green onions, white and green parts, diced

1/2 tablespoon coconut aminos

1/2 tablespoon Oyster Sauce (page 58)

1 teaspoon maple syrup

1/4 teaspoon white pepper

Sea salt

1 to 2 tablespoons Gratiam Jiaow (Deep-Fried Garlic, page 52), to serve

In a wok, heat 2 tablespoons of the oil over medium-high heat. Add the garlic and cauliflower rice or jasmine rice and stir-fry for 2 minutes.

Push the rice mixture to the side of the wok, add the remaining tablespoon of oil, and drop in the two eggs. Break the yolks and gently stir.

Let the eggs cook, break them apart with a spoon, and combine them with the rice mixture.

Add the green onions, coconut aminos, oyster sauce, maple syrup, and white pepper and stir-fry for another 30 seconds.

Season to taste with sea salt and serve topped with the deep-fried garlic.

Stir-Fried Rice Noodles

Pad Thai

A common street food in Thailand that's beloved by many here in the States, pad thai is a delicious concoction made with rice noodles, shrimp or chicken, ground peanuts, bean sprouts, and spices. Special thanks to Nusi, the owner and instructor at Silom Thai Cooking School in Bangkok, for teaching me how to create the unique and amazing taste that is pad thai.

To keep the flavors of authentic pad thai, I like to keep the spices the same but substitute cabbage for the rice noodles. It's still delicious, and it's more nutritious than the authentic version. But I've also included instructions for making this dish the traditional way, with rice noodles.

Prep time: 20 minutes

Cook time: 5 minutes

Serves: 2 to 3

8 ounces Thai rice noodles or 1 cup shredded green or napa cabbage

1 1/2 tablespoons coconut oil, palm oil, or leaf lard

3 cloves garlic, minced

2 teaspoons fish sauce

1 tablespoon Tamarind Paste (page 44) or rice vinegar

1 teaspoon maple syrup

5 to 6 medium prawns, shelled and deveined

1 egg, beaten

3 tablespoons diced green onions

2 tablespoons ground roasted cashews, for garnish

1 cup bean sprouts, plus additional for garnish

Dried red chili flakes, for garnish

Cilantro leaves, for garnish

With rice noodles

Bring a pot of water to a boil, place the rice noodles in a large glass bowl, and pour the boiling water over the noodles, just to cover. Let the noodles sit in the hot water for approximately 7 to 10 minutes, stirring every couple of minutes, until the noodles are soft but still al dente. Make sure they are not completely cooked because they will finish cooking during the stir-fry process. Drain immediately, rinse with cool water to stop the cooking process, and set aside.

In a wok, heat the oil over medium heat. Add the garlic and stir-fry until fragrant.

Add the cooked rice noodles and stir-fry, stirring quickly to make sure the noodles do not stick to each other or to the pan. Add more oil if needed.

Add the fish sauce, tamarind paste, and maple syrup, and mix well.

Push the noodles to the side of the wok and add the prawns. Sauté 2 minutes, or until they are pink and firm. Push the prawns aside and add the egg. Scramble the egg in the bottom of the wok until cooked through and mix together the prawns, noodles, and eggs.

Add the green onion and mix well. Garnish with the ground cashews, bean sprouts, dried chili flakes, and cilantro leaves and serve.

With cabbage

In a wok, heat the oil over medium heat. Add the garlic and stir-fry until fragrant.

Add the prawns, cabbage, and bean sprouts, and sauté 2 minutes, or until the prawns are pink and firm.

Add the egg and scramble it together with the rest of the ingredients.

Add the fish sauce, tamarind paste, maple syrup, and green onions. Mix well.

Garnish with the ground cashews, bean sprouts, dried red chili flakes, and cilantro leaves and serve.

Stir-Fried Flat Noodles

Pad See Ew

Another of my kids' favorites, this dish is traditionally made with wide rice noodles. Because rice does not bother us, we indulged in this dish from time to time during our travels. I now make the same recipe at home, sometimes with rice noodles and sometimes with zucchini noodles. The instructions here include both options.

Zucchini noodles can be made with a vegetable spiralizer or by slicing the zucchini with a mandoline and then cutting the slices in half again lengthwise to mimic the texture and size of rice noodles.

Prep time: 20 minutes

Cook time: 10 minutes

Serves: 2 to 3

2 tablespoons coconut oil

1 tablespoon minced shallots

1 tablespoon minced garlic

1/2 chicken breast, finely chopped

1 egg

1 cup fresh flat rice noodles, or 2 cups zucchini noodles

1 cup diced bok choy or kale

1 teaspoon coconut aminos

1/2 teaspoon fish sauce

1 teaspoon maple syrup

Heat the oil in a wok over medium-high heat. Add the shallots and garlic and stir-fry for a minute, just until the garlic is fragrant.

Add the chicken and stir-fry for 2 to 3 minutes, or just until almost cooked through.

If you're using rice noodles, add them to the wok and stir to break up the noodles.

Push the chicken to the side of the wok and add the egg. Break the yolk and cook the egg, mixing it with the chicken.

Add the zucchini noodles, bok choy, coconut aminos, fish sauce, and maple syrup. Stir for 1 to 2 minutes, or just until the bok choy is wilted. Taste and add more coconut aminos or fish sauce if needed.

Serve immediately.

Deep-Fried Omelet

Kao Load Kai
Jean Moo Sap

This was my breakfast staple while staying at Baan Pong, and it's so much fun to make. You can add whatever ingredients you like to jazz up this standard Thai fare. Try adding in shredded zucchini, minced garlic and chiles, or even cilantro to zest up your Thai omelet. I suggest serving this with Sweet Chili Sauce (page 72) or even Chile Oil (page 50).

Prep time: 10 minutes
Cook time: 4 to 5 minutes
Serves: 1 to 2

1/4 cup cooked ground pork or beef
2 eggs
3 teaspoons coconut aminos
2 tablespoons sliced green onions
1/2 teaspoon black pepper
1/2 cup palm shortening or leaf lard

In a bowl, mix together the ground pork, eggs, coconut aminos, green onions, and black pepper.

Melt the shortening in a wok until it's extremely hot and almost bubbling.

Pour the meat and egg mixture into the hot oil and let it fry until it's crispy on one side.

Flip and cook until the omelet is crispy on the other side. Flip a couple of times more to ensure that it's cooked all the way through.

Serve with Cauliflower Rice (page 40) or Sticky Rice (page 38) and Sweet Chili Sauce (page 72).

Stuffed
Egg Omelet

Eggs are a common part of any meal of the day in Thailand, and this classic stuffed omelet is a great option, especially if you're looking for something that isn't spicy. I've included chiles in this recipe because I like a little kick, but they're optional, and this omelet is just as scrumptious without them. Try different variations of this dish and serve topped with fresh herbs and Chile Oil (page 50) or Nam Pla Prik (Fish Sauce with Chiles, page 62). Thank you to Chef Jim at Baan Pong for teaching me how to make kai yat sai.

Kai Yat Sai

Prep time: 35 minutes

Cook time: 10 minutes

Serves: 2 to 3

Stuffing

1 tablespoon coconut oil, palm oil, or leaf lard

1/4 cup ground pork, beef, or chicken

1/4 cup finely chopped red or yellow bell pepper

1/4 cup finely chopped white onion

1/4 cup finely chopped tomato

1 to 3 small red or green Thai chiles, minced (optional)

1 clove garlic, minced

1/2 teaspoon maple syrup

2 to 3 teaspoons coconut aminos

1 teaspoon Oyster Sauce (page 58)

2 teaspoons tomato paste

1 teaspoon fish sauce

1 tablespoon chopped cilantro

1 tablespoon chopped sweet Thai basil

Sea salt and black pepper

Omelet

1/4 cup palm shortening or leaf lard

4 eggs

2 teaspoons coconut aminos

1 tablespoon chopped cilantro

1/4 teaspoon black pepper

To make the stuffing: Heat the oil in a wok over medium-high heat. Brown the meat and then add the remaining stuffing ingredients.

Stir-fry until the veggies are tender, about 3 to 4 minutes. Add salt and pepper to taste.

To make the omelet: In a separate omelet pan or wok, melt the palm shortening over medium heat.

While the oil is heating up, whisk together the omelet ingredients in a medium bowl.

Once the oil is hot, add the whisked omelet ingredients. Swirl the eggs gently around the pan like a crêpe, so that they coat the sides and the bottom of the pan.

Using your spatula, press the eggs down into the oil so that they become a little crispy on the bottom and cook all the way through.

Turn off the heat and place the stuffing mixture in the middle of the cooked egg.

Fold the sides of the omelet over the stuffing to create a square.

Gently remove the omelet from the pan, folded sides down. With a sharp knife, cut an opening in the top of the omelet to reveal the stuffing.

Garnish with cilantro leaves and serve with Chile Oil (page 50) or Nam Pla Prik (Fish Sauce with Chiles, page 62) if desired.

This is the authentic preparation for this dish. It can be a little challenging, so if it's easier to cook it as you would an ordinary omelet, that's fine, too—the flavors will be the same.

Sweet Chili Eggs

Khai Luuk Koei

Also known as "son-in-law eggs," you can find these fried hard-boiled eggs topped with a sweet and tangy tamarind sauce at street carts all over Thailand. I love to cook these at home and watch my boys' eyes get big as I drop whole hard-boiled eggs into hot oil and they puff and brown. They're so darn good topped with the thick, sticky sauce and dried chiles.

Prep time: 10 minutes

Cook time: 15 minutes

Serves: 3 to 4

1 cup palm shortening or leaf lard

5 hard-boiled eggs, peeled

2 tablespoons thinly sliced shallots or onions

2 tablespoons maple syrup

3 tablespoons Tamarind Paste (page 44) or rice vinegar

1 to 2 tablespoons fish sauce

4 to 5 small dried chiles

Cilantro leaves, for garnish

Heat the oil in a wok over medium-high heat.

Add the eggs to the hot oil and fry, turning occasionally, for approximately 4 to 5 minutes, or until golden brown.

Remove the eggs from the hot oil using a deep-fry skimmer and set aside.

Add the shallots to the hot oil and fry, stirring often, for about 1 minute, or until crispy. Remove with a deep-fry skimmer and set aside to drain.

In a small saucepan, mix together the maple syrup, tamarind paste, and fish sauce and bring to a simmer over medium heat.

Reduce the sauce, stirring constantly, for approximately 5 minutes, or until it has a syrup-like consistency.

Cut the eggs in half, place them on a plate, and drizzle the sauce over them. Top with the fried shallots and dried chiles and garnish with cilantro.

Try soft-boiling the eggs for this recipe; the richness of the runny yolk mixed with the sauce is delicious. To soft-boil eggs, place them in a small saucepan and cover with cold water; bring to a boil and let the eggs boil for 5 minutes. Remove the saucepan from the heat and immediately add ice cubes and hold under cold running water to stop the cooking process. Once the eggs are cool, peel and follow the directions to prepare the dish. Serve the eggs whole and drizzle the sauce over them so that when you cut into the eggs, the yolk mixes with the sauce.

Curries and Soups

Red Curry

Kaeng Ped

Red curry is my go-to meal whenever we eat at our favorite Thai restaurant here in Chico, and I made it myself at home several times before ever visiting Thailand, but as they say, it's always better straight from the source. I made my first curry paste for this dish while in Bangkok at Silom Thai Cooking School with my instructor Nusi, and it was such a pleasure to cook with a paste and coconut milk that I made myself. To make this traditional dish all from scratch is truly an art, and it's well worth the time. Of course, it's also delicious when made with store-bought curry paste and coconut milk, so don't skip this one just because you are short on time; it can be made quickly as well!

Prep time: 15 minutes (+ 45 minutes if preparing your own curry paste)

Cook time: 10 minutes

Serves: 2 to 3

2 tablespoons coconut oil, palm oil, or leaf lard

1 to 2 tablespoons Red Curry Paste (page 55)

1/2 pound thinly sliced chicken breast, pork loin, or beef

2 cups Coconut Milk (page 32)

1/4 cup thinly sliced ginger, cut into matchstick-sized pieces

1 tablespoon fish sauce

1 to 2 tablespoons Tamarind Paste (page 44) or vinegar

1 teaspoon maple syrup

5 to 6 Thai eggplants, quartered, or 1 cup sliced Japanese eggplant

6 kaffir lime leaves, torn into quarters

1 medium red Thai chile, sliced, plus more for garnish

20 leaves sweet Thai basil, plus more for garnish

Heat the oil in a wok over medium-high heat.

Add the curry paste and cook, stirring frequently, for about 30 seconds, or until fragrant.

Add the meat and stir-fry it with the curry paste and oil just until coated.

Turn the heat up to high, pour in the coconut milk, and bring to a boil. Once you see the fat separating on the sides, turn the heat down to medium and let the curry simmer for another few seconds.

Add the ginger, fish sauce, tamarind paste, and maple syrup. Taste and adjust the seasoning as needed.

Add the eggplant, kaffir lime leaves, chile, and basil, and bring back to a boil for 2 to 3 minutes.

Serve immediately with Cauliflower Rice (page 40) or Jasmine Rice (page 36). Garnish with more basil and sliced chiles if desired.

Yellow Curry

Kaeng Karii

Yellow curry is my son Coby's favorite Thai dish, and I missed him terribly every time I ate it in Thailand, since he was unable to join us on the trip. But now I can make the real deal for him at home, and it's such a joy to see how much he enjoys this authentic version of his favorite Thai dish.

Prep time: 30 minutes (+ 45 minutes if preparing your own curry paste)

Cook time: 25 minutes

Serves: 2 to 3

1 cup peeled and cubed white potato or sweet potato

1 tablespoon coconut or palm oil

1 tablespoon Yellow Curry Paste (page 55)

1 pound large prawns, chicken breast, pork loin, or beef, thinly sliced

1/2 yellow onion, coarsely chopped

1 cup Coconut Milk (page 32)

1 tablespoon Tamarind Paste (page 44)

2 tablespoons fish sauce

2 teaspoons maple syrup

1/2 cup sliced red bell pepper

1 kaffir lime leaf, chiffonaded

Sweet Thai basil leaves, for garnish

Bring a small pot of water to a boil. Add the potatoes and parboil for about 5 minutes. Drain and set aside.

In another soup pot or wok, heat the oil over medium-high heat. Stir in the curry paste and cook for about 30 seconds, or just until fragrant.

Add the chicken, pork or beef, potatoes, onion, coconut milk, tamarind paste, fish sauce, and maple syrup, and mix well.

Bring to a simmer and cook for approximately 7 to 10 minutes, or until the potatoes are soft and the meat is cooked through and tender. Add the red bell peppers and cook for another minute. If using prawns, add them with the red bell peppers once the potatoes are fork-tender and cook for another 3 to 5 minutes, or until the prawns are pink and firm.

Add more coconut milk if the sauce becomes too thick, and season with more fish sauce, tamarind paste, and maple syrup to taste.

Add the kaffir lime leaf, stir, and garnish with basil leaves. Serve with Cauliflower Rice (page 40) or Jasmine Rice (page 36).

Green Curry

Green curry was always one of my favorite Thai dishes at restaurants in the States, and eating authentic gang keow waan in Thailand was not a disappointment. There are several varieties of eggplant in Thailand, and I was surprised at first to encounter pea eggplant, a tiny, green, pea-sized eggplant, in almost all the green curries that I ate there. This dish does need eggplant, but feel free to use the easier-to-find Japanese eggplant instead.

Kaeng Keow Waan

Prep time: 20 minutes (+ 45 minutes if preparing your own curry paste)

Cook time: 10 minutes

Serves: 2 to 3

1 tablespoon coconut or palm oil

2 tablespoons Green Curry Paste (page 55)

1/2 pound chicken breast, pork loin, or beef, thinly sliced

1 cup Coconut Milk (page 32)

1/2 cup water

1/2 to 1 tablespoon maple syrup

Sea salt

1/2 cup pea eggplant or sliced Japanese eggplant

4 small red Thai chiles, halved

3 to 4 kaffir lime leaves, torn in half

Small handful of sweet Thai basil leaves

Heat the oil in a wok over medium-high to high heat. Add the green curry paste and stir to make a paste with the oil.

Add the meat to the wok and stir-fry in the curry paste just until the meat is coated in the paste.

Turn the heat up to high and add the coconut milk and water.

Add the maple syrup and sea salt to taste and gently mix.

Bring to a rapid boil and add the eggplant, chiles, and kaffir lime leaves. Continue to boil rapidly for another minute.

Add the basil leaves. Stir and let simmer for about 15 seconds, just until the leaves wilt.

Serve immediately with Cauliflower Rice (page 40) or Jasmine Rice (page 36).

Massaman Curry

Kaeng Matsaman

This special curry has a very distinct Middle Eastern flavor from the cardamom and cinnamon. Legend has it that this is a Muslim-influenced dish that should never be made with pork, although now and then you will see it prepared that way. Kaeng matsaman is inherently less spicy than other Thai curries and is often made for children who are not yet used to the heat that is prominent in most Thai dishes.

Prep time: 20 minutes

Cook time: 15 minutes

Serves: 2 to 3

2 tablespoons coconut oil or leaf lard

3 tablespoons Massaman Curry Paste (page 56)

1 pound chicken or beef, cut into 1-inch cubes

1 small sweet potato, cut into 2-inch cubes (about 1/2 cup)

1/2 cup chopped white onion

2 cups Coconut Milk (page 32)

2 dried bay leaves

3 cardamom pods

1 (1-inch) stick cinnamon

3 to 4 tablespoons fish sauce

2 to 3 tablespoons maple syrup

1 1/2 tablespoons Tamarind Paste (page 44)

1/4 cup roasted cashews

In a soup pot or wok, heat the oil over medium-high heat.

Add the curry paste and mix with the oil for about 15 seconds, just until fragrant and sizzling. Add the meat and sweet potatoes and stir until coated in the curry paste.

Add the coconut milk, turn the heat up to high, and wait until the fat starts to separate on the edges of the pot and the milk starts to boil.

Mix well until the curry is blended into the coconut milk.

Add the bay leaves, cardamom pods, and cinnamon stick. Turn the heat down to low or medium-low and let simmer for about 7 to 10 minutes, until the potatoes are tender.

Season with the fish sauce, maple syrup, and tamarind paste. Taste and add more if desired.

Add the cashews, stir, and serve immediately with Cauliflower Rice (page 40) or Jasmine Rice (page 36).

Duck Curry with Fresh Fruit

If you like duck, you will love this curry dish. From using the rendered duck fat to fry the curry paste to adding fresh fruit, it's an unusual and very special recipe. Duck is one of the favorite foods of Mike, our dear friend, travel companion, and photographer, and I loved watching him enjoy this amazing meal—almost as much as I loved eating it!

Kaeng Ped Phed Yaang

Prep time: 35 minutes

Cook time: 20 minutes

Serves: 2 to 3

1 duck breast

1 tablespoon Red Curry Paste (page 55)

1 1/2 to 2 cups Coconut Milk (page 32)

4 kaffir lime leaves, 2 torn into quarters and 2 chiffonaded

1 medium red Thai chile, cut in half lengthwise, seeded, and julienned

1 cup chopped pineapple

1 cup halved green or purple grapes

1 cup halved cherry tomatoes

2 to 3 teaspoons fish sauce

1 to 2 tablespoons maple syrup

2 bunches sweet Thai basil leaves

Score the skin of the duck breast and sear in a dry, hot skillet skin side down. Flip once the skin is browned and sear for another minute or two on the other side.

Remove the duck breast from the skillet and set aside.

Pour the rendered duck fat from searing the breast into a soup pot or wok and heat over medium-high heat.

Add the curry paste to the hot duck fat and stir together for about 15 seconds, just until fragrant.

Pour in the coconut milk, mix well, and bring to a boil for a minute or two.

Add the duck breast, kaffir lime leaves, and chile to the coconut milk mixture, turn the heat down to medium-low, and let simmer, covered if possible, for 10 minutes.

Remove the duck breast from the curry and slice.

Add the pineapple, grapes, tomatoes, fish sauce, and maple syrup to the coconut milk mixture. Taste and add more fish sauce and maple syrup if desired.

Add the sliced duck breast back to the curry along with the basil leaves, mix well, and let simmer for 1 minute. Serve immediately with Cauliflower Rice (page 40) or Jasmine Rice (page 36).

Panaeng Curry

Kaeng Panang

There are no words to describe how simply scrumptious this curry is. It was, by far, the favorite of my ten-year-old son, Jaden. I ordered panaeng curry every chance I could, and of course it had to be a part of this book. While it's not as spicy as other traditional Thai curries, panaeng curry has such a richness and depth of flavor that it's surprising there are so few ingredients. It's all about the quality of the curry paste and the care that goes into the simple yet ingenious creation of this dish. I first made this with Chef Jim while staying at Baan Pong and immediately fell in love.

Prep time: 10 minutes

Cook time: 7 to 10 minutes

Serves: 2 to 3

1 tablespoon coconut oil, palm oil, or leaf lard

2 tablespoons Panaeng Curry Paste (page 55)

1/2 pound chicken breast, beef, or pork loin, cut into thinly sliced bite-sized pieces (about 1 cup)

1 cup Coconut Milk (page 32)

1 tablespoon maple syrup

Sea salt

Heat the oil in a wok over medium-high heat.

Add the curry paste to the hot oil and stir for about 15 seconds, just until fragrant and sizzling.

Add the meat to the wok and stir-fry until it is coated with the curry paste.

Turn the heat to high and add the coconut milk. After the milk starts to boil and you see the fat separating from the milk, stir until well combined.

Add the maple syrup and salt to taste and cook for another 4 to 5 minutes, or until the meat is done all the way through.

Serve with Cauliflower Rice (page 40) or Jasmine Rice (page 36).

Northern-Style Slow-Cooked Pork

Kaeng Hung Ley

Most Thai dishes are quick to prepare, but this is slow-cooked pork made on the stovetop, and it's a labor of love. The spicy red curry mixed with the distinct taste of yellow curry powder is a gift to this dish, which is a staple favorite in northern Thailand.

Prep time: 30 minutes or overnight to marinate

Cook time: 2 hours 15 minutes

Serves: 2 to 3

1 tablespoon Red Curry Paste (page 55)

2 teaspoons curry powder

1 teaspoon coconut aminos

1 pound pork roast, cut into bite-sized cubes

4 cups chicken broth

1 to 2 cups water

1/2 ounce ginger, cut into matchstick-sized pieces

4 to 5 cloves garlic, peeled and lightly crushed with the flat side of a knife

2 tablespoons roasted cashews

1 teaspoon Tamarind Paste (page 44)

1 tablespoon maple syrup

1/2 tablespoon fish sauce

Sea salt

In a medium bowl, mix together the red curry paste, curry powder, and coconut aminos. Add the pork to the bowl and mix until the pork is coated with the curry mixture. Refrigerate the pork overnight or for at least 30 minutes.

In a large dry wok or soup pot, cook the pork over medium-high heat for 3 to 4 minutes, just until the outside of the pork is seared.

Add the chicken broth to the wok and bring to boil. Turn the heat down to low and simmer, uncovered, until the pork is tender, about 2 hours. Add the water a little at a time as needed to make sure the pork is always covered with liquid.

Add the ginger, garlic, and cashews. Add the tamarind paste, maple syrup, fish sauce, and sea salt to taste.

Simmer for another 10 to 15 minutes, or until the pork is fork-tender.

Southern Pork with Yellow Curry

Keang Kati
Look Liang Moo

This is not the typical yellow curry that you might find in a Thai restaurant in the States; it's an authentic, southern-style curry that's made with a combination of shrimp paste, yellow curry paste, and the amazing stink bean! I of course offer you a substitute for the stink beans—green beans will work just as well. Thank you so much to Bow of A.O Seafood Restaurant in Khao Lak for one of our most memorable days in Thailand.

Prep time: 10 minutes

Cook time: 10 to 12 minutes

Serves: 2 to 3

1/2 cup chicken broth

1 1/2 cups Coconut Milk (page 32)

1 teaspoon shrimp paste

1 tablespoon Yellow Curry Paste (page 55)

3 kaffir lime leaves, stemmed and torn into quarters

2 teaspoons maple syrup

7 ounces pork loin, cut into 1/4-inch cubes

1 cup sprouted stink beans or green beans

In a wok over high heat, bring the chicken broth and coconut milk to a boil.

Add the shrimp paste and curry paste and mix well.

Add the kaffir lime leaves and maple syrup, mix, and let simmer for 5 minutes.

Add the pork and stink beans and simmer for another 5 to 7 minutes, or until pork is tender and done all the way through.

Serve immediately with Cauliflower Rice (page 40) or Jasmine Rice (page 36).

Spicy Northern Curry

Kaeng Khane

This curry from northern Thailand is not the creamy curry that's served at most restaurants in the States. Gang khane has a real spicy kick from the red curry, and the small Thai chiles push the heat factor even higher. If you are sensitive to very spicy foods, omit the chiles and start with 1 tablespoon of curry and add more if you need to at the end. This dish isn't just about the heat, though; the fresh cilantro, tender eggplant, and crunchy green beans all combine for a tasty curry.

Prep time: 20 minutes

Cook time: 7 minutes

Serves: 2 to 3

1 tablespoon palm oil, coconut oil, or leaf lard

2 to 3 tablespoons Red Curry Paste (page 55)

1/2 pound pork loin, beef, or chicken, thinly sliced (about 1 cup)

1 1/2 cups chicken broth

Sea salt

1 teaspoon maple syrup

4 to 5 Thai eggplants, quartered, or 1 Japanese eggplant, cut into 2-inch pieces

1/2 cup coarsely chopped green beans or long beans

1/2 cup sliced straw or crimini mushrooms

2 to 5 small red Thai chiles

1/4 cup chopped cilantro

Heat the oil in a wok over medium-high heat.

Mix the red curry paste into the oil and let sizzle for about 15 seconds, until fragrant.

Add the meat and coat it in the curry paste. Stir-fry for 1 to 2 minutes.

Add the chicken broth, salt to taste, and maple syrup and mix well.

Add the eggplant, green beans, mushrooms, and chiles. Bring to a rapid boil, then turn the heat down and simmer for 1 to 3 minutes.

Top with the cilantro and serve.

Northern-Style Curry

Khao Soi

Khao soi is a much-loved traditional soup from northern Thailand. Everyone makes khao soi just a little bit differently, but what makes it khao soi is the use of egg noodles and the distinct hint of yellow curry powder added to the red curry paste. The traditional dish is made with egg noodles and topped with deep-fried egg noodles, pickled cabbage, diced shallots, and a squeeze of lime juice. This version is similar to the original, but I suggest using sweet potato "noodles" made with a vegetable spiralizer (see page 27) instead of wheat-based egg noodles in order to keep it grain-free.

Prep time: 30 minutes

Cook time: 15 minutes

Serves: 2 to 3

Crispy Noodle Topping (optional)

3/4 cup palm shortening or leaf lard

1/2 cup sweet potato noodles

2 tablespoons coconut oil

2 tablespoons Khao Soi Curry Paste (page 55)

1/4 pound chicken breast, cut into thinly sliced bite-sized pieces (about 1/2 cup)

1 cup Coconut Milk (page 32)

1/4 to 1/2 cup chicken broth

1 cup sweet potato noodles

2 to 3 teaspoons maple syrup

Sea salt

Diced shallots, for garnish

Pickled cabbage, for garnish

Cilantro leaves, for garnish

Chile Oil (page 50), for garnish

Lime wedges, for garnish

To make the topping: Melt the palm shortening in a small saucepan and heat until it's hot enough to sizzle when you add the sweet potato noodles. Drop in the noodles and fry, turning often, until brown and crispy. Remove and set aside to drain.

To make the curry: In a wok, heat the coconut oil over medium-high heat. Stir the curry paste into the oil and sauté for about 15 seconds, until fragrant and sizzling.

Add the chicken and stir-fry in the curry and oil just until the chicken is coated, about 10 seconds.

Add the coconut milk and do not stir until the milk begins to boil and the fat from the coconut milk begins to separate around the edges. Then stir to blend the curry into the coconut milk.

Let simmer for 1 minute.

Add the chicken broth and sweet potato noodles and let simmer for another 4 to 5 minutes, or until the noodles are tender.

Add the maple syrup and sea salt to taste.

Serve garnished with the shallots, pickled cabbage, cilantro leaves, chile oil, and lime wedges and topped with the Crispy Noodle Topping.

Southern Sour Curry

Kaeng Som

Sour curry? Really? Those were my exact thoughts when Ninja started making this dish in Bangkok at Enjoy Bistro. When I think of Thai curry, I think sweet, spicy, creamy—not sour! However, this authentic southern Thai dish is not just amazing but different, tantalizing, fun, and absolutely worth making. It's not commonly found in Thai restaurants in America, and it uses a very interesting ingredient called Acacia pennata, which looks almost like a fern and tastes similar to bok choy or spinach. Make kaeng som for a Thai dinner party and impress your friends with your knowledge of regional Thai cuisine.

Prep time: 30 minutes

Cook time: 20 minutes

Serves: 2 to 3

3 tablespoons coconut oil or palm oil

2 eggs

3/4 cup *Acacia pennata* or finely chopped bok choy leaves, spinach, or kale

2 cups water

2 tablespoons Southern Sour Curry Paste (page 56)

1 to 3 tablespoons maple syrup

2 tablespoons Garlic-Infused Vinegar (page 42)

3 tablespoons Tamarind Paste (page 44)

1 teaspoon fish sauce

Sea salt

1 small carrot, chopped

5 large prawns

Cilantro, for garnish

Celery leaves or green onion stems, for garnish

Heat the oil in a wok over medium-high heat. While it heats, in a small bowl whisk together the eggs and *Acacia pennata*.

Pour the egg mixture into the hot oil. Cook it as you would an omelet, without scrambling the eggs. Flip once it's brown and crispy. As it cooks, press it down with a spatula to ensure it cooks all the way through.

Remove the omelet and set aside to drain.

Add the water to a soup pot and bring almost to a boil.

Add the curry paste to the water and stir until blended.

Add the maple syrup, vinegar, tamarind paste, fish sauce, and sea salt. Taste and add more seasoning if necessary.

Add the carrot and prawns and cook for about 3 to 4 minutes.

While the carrots and prawns are cooking, cut the omelet into 2-inch pieces and place in the bottom of a large soup bowl.

Once the prawns are pink and firm, remove from heat and pour the soup over the omelet in the bowl.

Garnish with cilantro and celery leaves.

Boiled Rice Soup

Kao Tom

This was one of the kids' favorite meals while we were staying at the beautiful Baan Pong and cooking with Chef Jim in her tiny outdoor kitchen. Now that we are home, I make this dish with either Cauliflower Rice (page 40) or the standard white rice. The poached egg adds the perfect touch to this Thai comfort food. Try spicing up this mild soup with a few drops of Chile Oil (page 50) or Nam Pla Prik (Fish Sauce with Chiles, page 62).

Prep time: 15 minutes (+ 30 minutes to prepare the deep-fried garlic)

Cook time: 10 minutes

Serves: 2 to 3

1 cup chicken broth

1 cup water

1/2 cup ground pork or shredded cooked chicken breast

1 teaspoon coconut aminos

1/4 teaspoon black pepper, plus more to taste

1 cup Cauliflower Rice (page 40), uncooked, or 1 cup cooked Jasmine Rice (page 36)

Sea salt

1 egg

1 tablespoon Gratiam Jiaow (Deep-Fried Garlic, page 52), for garnish

2 green onions, tips only, sliced, for garnish

Chile Oil (page 50; optional)

Nam Pla Prik (Fish Sauce with Chiles, page 62; optional)

In a saucepan or small soup pot, heat the chicken broth and water until simmering.

If using ground pork, in a small bowl mix together the ground pork, coconut aminos, and black pepper.

Using your hands, pinch out small meatballs (about the size of marbles) of the pork mixture and drop them into the simmering broth.

Add the cauliflower or jasmine rice and gently stir.

If using chicken breast instead of pork, add the chicken with the cauliflower rice once the broth starts to simmer.

Simmer until the pork meatballs are done all the way through, about 5 minutes, or, if using chicken, for 3 to 4 minutes, until the chicken and cauliflower rice are hot.

Season the soup to taste with salt and pepper.

Add an egg in the middle of the soup and let it poach in the simmering liquid.

Once the white of the egg is done, serve the soup in a bowl topped with the deep-fried garlic and green onion tips.

Add a few drops of chile oil or nam pla prik if desired.

Savory Glass Noodle Soup

Gaing Joot Woon Sen

This soup is traditionally made with glass noodles, which are made from mung beans and are naturally gluten-free. If you can tolerate legumes, you can use glass noodles to make this dish entirely authentic, but if you want to avoid all starch, try zucchini noodles instead—in my opinion, they are actually more flavorful, and they are most definitely more nutritious! We had this soup on several occasions while in Thailand and it was a sure favorite among the kids. I suggest adding a bit of spice with Chile Oil (page 50) before serving.

Prep time: 30 minutes

Cook time: 8 to 10 minutes

Serves: 2 to 3

2 cups chicken broth

1 cup water

1/2 cup ground pork, beef, or chicken

1 teaspoon coconut aminos

1/2 teaspoon black pepper, plus more to taste

1/2 cup sliced carrots

1/2 cup chopped celery

2 teaspoons coconut aminos

1/2 cup sliced straw or white mushrooms

1 cup shredded cabbage

2 green onion stems, cut into long pieces

1 medium zucchini, cut into noodles with a vegetable spiralizer (about 1 cup)

Cilantro leaves, for garnish (optional)

Chile Oil (page 50), for garnish (optional)

In a small soup pot, bring the chicken broth and water to a simmer over medium-high heat.

While the broth is heating, combine the meat, coconut aminos, and black pepper in a small bowl.

Once the broth is hot, drop in small meatballs (about the size of a marble) of the meat mixture and let simmer for 3 to 4 minutes.

Add the carrots and celery and simmer for 1 minute.

Add the coconut aminos, taste, and add more if needed.

Add the mushrooms, cabbage, and green onions and simmer for another 3 to 4 minutes. Add black pepper to taste.

Place the zucchini noodles in a large soup bowl and pour the hot soup over the noodles.

Garnish with cilantro leaves and chile oil if desired and serve immediately.

Sweet and Sour Chicken and Coconut Soup

Tom Ka Gai

This is Thai comfort food at its finest. I love—adore, actually—this simple, delicious, sweet and tangy soup. There is something truly magical about the sweetness of coconut milk, the tartness of kaffir lime leaves, and the light, delightful flavor of lemongrass, and this soup harnesses all of these amazing ingredients to yield a burst of flavor in every spoonful.

Prep time: 30 minutes

Cook time: 7 to 10 minutes

Serves: 2

1 cup Coconut Milk (page 32)

1 cup chicken broth or water

1 stalk lemongrass, cut into 1-inch pieces (bend the stalk in several places prior to cutting to release the flavor)

1 tablespoon thinly sliced galangal

3 straw or white mushrooms, quartered

3 to 4 kaffir lime leaves, stemmed and torn in half

1/2 chicken breast, chopped

1 teaspoon maple syrup

Sea salt

1/4 white onion, chopped (about 1/3 cup)

1 small tomato, chopped (about 1/3 cup)

1 1/2 tablespoons lime juice

Chopped cilantro, for garnish (optional)

Chile Oil (page 50), for garnish (optional)

In a wok or soup pot, bring the coconut milk and chicken broth to a boil.

Add the lemongrass, galangal, mushrooms, kaffir lime leaves, and chicken and stir well.

To the simmering soup, add the maple syrup and salt to taste, stir, and add the onion and tomato.

Cook over high heat, stirring occasionally, until the chicken is cooked through, about 3 to 5 minutes.

Remove from heat and add the lime juice. Taste and adjust the seasoning as desired.

Garnish with the cilantro and chile oil if desired and serve.

Clear Spicy Soup

Tom Sab

This soup from the Isaan region of Thailand reminds me a little of Chinese hot and sour soup, but it's so much better. Feel free to substitute thinly sliced beef, chicken, or even prawns for the pork if you like. I prefer pork because this flavorful meat really enhances the taste of the soup.

Prep time: 30 minutes

Cook time: 8 minutes

Serves: 2 to 3

2 cups water

4 kaffir lime leaves, torn into quarters

2 medium red or green Thai chiles, cut in half lengthwise

1 lemongrass stalk, cut into 1/8-inch pieces

1/4 cup sliced shallots

1 (1-inch) piece galangal, thinly sliced

1/2 pound boneless pork ribs, cut into 1/4-inch-thick pieces

1 tablespoon sesame oil

1 teaspoon sea salt

1 tablespoon Oyster Sauce (page 58)

2 tablespoons Garlic-Infused Vinegar (page 42)

1 tablespoon Tamarind Paste (page 44)

3 straw or crimini mushrooms, quartered

2 small tomatoes, quartered

1 tablespoon Khao Koor (Toasted Rice Powder, page 46)

1/4 cup chopped cilantro or sawtooth coriander

1/4 cup holy or sweet Thai basil leaves, torn in half

In a saucepan or small soup pot, add the water, kaffir lime leaves, chiles, lemongrass, shallots, and galangal.

Bring to a boil over medium-high heat and add the pork.

Add the sesame oil, sea salt, oyster sauce, vinegar, and tamarind paste, and mix well.

Turn the heat down to medium and add the mushrooms and tomatoes.

Let simmer for 4 to 5 minutes, or until the pork is tender and no longer pink.

Add the rice powder, cilantro, and basil leaves. Mix just to blanch the herbs and serve immediately.

Creamy Hot and Sour Prawn Soup

Tom Yum Goong

This delicious, fresh, and delightful soup can be made with any kind of meat, but the combination of fresh prawns, the spicy sweetness of the soup, the fresh taste of lime and lemongrass, and the subtle creaminess of the coconut milk is nothing short of divine. I made this soup with Nusi at his cooking school during our first full day in Bangkok, and after one bite, I knew this was the beginning of a culinary trip of a lifetime.

Prep time: 30 minutes

Cook time: 15 minutes

Serves: 2 to 3

1 1/2 cups chicken broth

1 stalk lemongrass, tough outer layer removed, cut into 2-inch pieces

3 kaffir lime leaves, torn in half

1 (2-inch) piece of galangal, sliced into thin pieces

2 to 3 small red Thai chiles, stemmed and cut in half lengthwise

5 to 7 medium prawns, shelled and deveined

5 to 6 cherry tomatoes, halved

4 to 5 small white mushrooms, quartered

2 teaspoons fish sauce

1 teaspoon lime juice, plus more to taste

1 tablespoon chopped fresh cilantro leaves

1 tablespoon chopped green onions

1 teaspoon Nam Prik Pao (Thai Chili Paste, page 64)

2 to 3 tablespoons Coconut Milk (page 32)

In a small saucepan, combine the chicken broth, lemongrass, kaffir lime leaves, galangal, and chiles. Bring to a boil, then turn down to a simmer for 10 minutes.

Add the prawns and simmer for 2 to 3 minutes, just until they're pink and tender.

Add the tomatoes, fish sauce, lime juice, cilantro, green onions, chili paste, and coconut milk. Gently mix, simmer for another minute, and serve.

Shrimp with Pak Miang Leaves in Coconut Milk

Pak Miang Tom Kati Koong Sot

After his first bite of this dish, our friend and photographer Mike looked up, startled, and said, "Wow, this is like Thai clam chowder!" He was totally right. The surprising sweetness and creaminess of this dish combines with the shrimp paste, pak miang leaves, and fresh shrimp to give it that familiar clam chowder taste, but with a Thai twist. This is a famous southern Thai dish that is said to be the favorite food of Thai princess Maha Chakri Sirindhom, and one she always orders when visiting southern Thailand. It's definitely worth traveling for, but the good news is that you can make pak miang tom kati koong sot right at home in your own kitchen. I substitute spinach for the pak miang leaves, and the result is stunningly similar to the authentic version.

Prep time: 10 minutes

Cook time: 7 minutes

Serves: 2 to 3

1 1/2 cups Coconut Milk (page 32)

1/2 cup chicken broth

1 1/2 teaspoons shrimp paste

2 teaspoons maple syrup

1/4 cup chopped white onion

10 small shrimp, shells and tails removed and deveined

1 1/2 cups pak miang or spinach leaves

Sea salt

Add the coconut milk and chicken broth to a small soup pot and bring to a boil over medium-high heat.

Add the shrimp paste, maple syrup, and white onion, stir well, and let simmer for 3 to 4 minutes.

Add the shrimp and pak miang leaves and simmer for another 2 to 3 minutes, until the shrimp are pink and firm and the spinach is wilted.

Taste, season with salt if needed, and serve.

Sour and Spicy Prawn with Lemongrass Soup

Dtom Yum Goong

This soup comes straight from Pom's amazing Cooking@home Thai Culinary School in Chiang Mai, and it tastes just like it should: homemade and from the heart. This is a fresh, herb-filled broth packed with vegetables and prawns. It's truly a favorite of mine.

Prep time: 30 minutes

Cook time: 7 to 10 minutes

Serves: 2 to 3

1 cup chicken broth

1 cup water

2 stalks lemongrass, tough outer layer removed, cut into 1- to 2-inch pieces

4 kaffir lime leaves, stemmed and torn into quarters

5 thin slices galangal

2 cloves garlic, smashed and cut in half

2 to 6 small red Thai chiles, pounded into a paste in a wooden mortar and pestle

1/4 cup sliced onions

3 straw or crimini mushrooms, quartered

4 to 5 prawns, shelled and deveined

4 to 5 cherry tomatoes, halved

1 tablespoon fish sauce

1 tablespoon chopped cilantro stems

1 tablespoon lime juice

Cilantro leaves, for garnish

In a soup pot or wok, bring the chicken broth and water to a boil.

Add the lemongrass, kaffir lime leaves, galangal, garlic, chiles, and onions. Simmer for 3 to 5 minutes.

Add the mushrooms and boil for 1 minute.

Add the prawns, tomatoes, fish sauce, cilantro stems, and lime juice, and simmer for another 2 to 3 minutes, until the prawns are pink and firm.

Taste and adjust seasoning as needed.

Garnish with fresh cilantro leaves and serve.

Stir-Fry and Seafood

Sweet Basil Leaf Stir-Fry

Pad Krapow

The smell of fresh Thai basil is seriously intoxicating. Hit the wok with some hot chiles, fresh vegetables, and a succulent sauce, stir in a handful of basil, and really, that's all you need to amaze your friends and family. You can find this stir-fry in restaurants all over Thailand, and I ate it at Baan Pong in Chiang Mai often enough to know that it's one of my favorites.

Prep time: 30 minutes

Cook time: 5 minutes

Serves: 2 to 3

3 cloves garlic, peeled

5 to 6 small red or green Thai chiles, stemmed

1 tablespoon coconut oil, palm oil, or leaf lard

1/2 pound chicken, beef, or pork, thinly sliced (about 1 cup), or 10 small shrimp

1 to 2 tablespoons chicken broth or water

1/4 cup finely diced carrots

1/4 cup finely diced green beans

2 to 3 medium red or green Thai chiles, sliced

2 tablespoons coconut aminos

1 tablespoon Oyster Sauce (page 58)

1 teaspoon maple syrup

Sea salt and black pepper

1/2 cup sweet Thai basil leaves, plus more for garnish

Lime wedges, for garnish

Place the garlic and small chiles in a wooden mortar and pestle and pound until broken down.

Heat the oil in a wok over medium heat. Once hot, add the garlic and chile mixture and stir-fry for about 30 seconds, just until fragrant.

Add the chicken, beef, or pork and stir-fry for another 30 seconds.

Add the chicken broth and stir. The mixture should be hot and sizzling.

Add the carrots, green beans, medium chiles, coconut aminos, oyster sauce, and maple syrup. Add salt and pepper to taste and stir-fry for another 1 to 2 minutes, or until the meat is done all the way through and tender.

If using shrimp, add the carrots, green beans, and medium chiles first, stir-fry for 1 to 2 minutes, and then add the shrimp, chicken broth, coconut aminos, oyster sauce, and maple syrup. Add salt and pepper to taste and stir-fry for 1 to 2 minutes, until the shrimp are pink and firm.

Add the basil leaves and stir just until wilted.

Garnish with a few more fresh basil leaves and lime wedges, and serve.

Crab and Yellow Curry Stir-Fry

Boo Paht Pong Karee

We ate this dish for the first time at Enjoy Bistro in Bangkok, where it was served with whole blue crabs, shells and all. These succulent little crabs are not easy to find, which made it difficult to re-create this dish. Let's be honest: it simply isn't always possible to find exactly what you want to re-create a dish that is out-of-this-world delicious. But you can get darn close, and that's what this recipe is all about—getting as close as possible without hopping on the next plane to Thailand in order to find the real deal. The succulent sweetness of the crab combined with the richness of the curry powder is completely worth it. I suggest using soft-shell crab if you can find it, but fresh crab meat or, really, any seafood of your choice will work.

Prep time: 20 minutes

Cook time: 5 minutes

Serves: 2 to 3

2 teaspoons Chile Oil (page 50)

Pinch of sea salt

1 egg

2 tablespoons coconut or palm oil

5 small soft-shell crabs, or about 1/2 pound fresh crab meat or seafood of your choice (such as prawns or finely chopped white fish)

1/2 tablespoon plus 1/2 teaspoon yellow curry powder, divided

2 tablespoons plus 1/4 cup Coconut Milk (page 32), divided

1 1/2 tablespoons Oyster Sauce (page 58)

1/2 tablespoon maple syrup

1/2 teaspoon sea salt

1/4 cup chopped white onion

1 medium red Thai chile, cut into thirds

1 green onion, cut into 1-inch pieces

1/4 cup celery leaves, for garnish

In a small bowl, whisk together the chile oil, sea salt, and egg.

Heat a wok over high heat; once hot, add the coconut oil.

Add the egg mixture to the wok and stir immediately, turning the heat down to medium or medium-high.

Add the crab, 1/2 tablespoon of the curry powder, 1 tablespoon of the coconut milk, the oyster sauce, maple syrup, and sea salt, and stir-fry together for 1 minute.

Add the remaining coconut milk and the remaining 1/2 teaspoon of curry powder and turn up the heat to high.

Add the onion, medium chile, and green onion and stir-fry for another minute.

Garnish with celery leaves and serve.

Stir-Fry Fish with Celery

Crunchy, saucy, and just a touch spicy, this dish is glorious. I ate it in Bangkok and didn't see it again anywhere else, but from what I understand, it's most commonly cooked at home rather than at street carts or in restaurants. Make sure the fish is very fresh and deboned before you make this wonderful meal.

Pla Pad Keun Chai

Prep time: 30 minutes
Cook time: 15 minutes
Serves: 2 to 3

Tempura Batter

1/2 cup tapioca flour

2 tablespoons sparkling water

1 egg

Pinch of sea salt

2 cups palm shortening or leaf lard

2 small fillets cod or other mild white fish (about 1 pound), cut into pieces 2 inches long and 1/4 inch thick

2 cloves garlic

1 tablespoon coconut or palm oil

1/4 cup Chinese celery or 2 celery ends with leaves, cut into 2-inch pieces

2 green onions, white and green parts, cut into 2-inch pieces

2 medium red Thai chiles, cut in half lengthwise

1 tablespoon Oyster Sauce (page 58)

1 tablespoon Nam Prik Pao (Thai Chili Paste, page 64)

1 tablespoon fish sauce

1/2 to 1 teaspoon maple syrup

3 tablespoons chicken broth

In a small bowl, combine the ingredients for the tempura batter.

Melt the shortening in a wok over high heat and heat until very hot. While it heats, coat the fish in the tempura batter.

Once the oil is hot enough to sizzle when you add the fish, gently slide in the battered fish and fry for about 2 to 3 minutes, turning often, until the outside is golden and crispy.

Remove the fish and set aside to drain.

Remove the oil from the wok and reserve if desired for later use. In a wooden mortar and pestle, smash the garlic with the coconut oil.

Add the garlic and oil mixture to the wok and turn the heat up to high.

Once the oil and garlic are sizzling and fragrant, which will only take a few seconds, add the celery, green onions, and chiles and stir.

Add the oyster sauce, chili paste, fish sauce, maple syrup, and chicken broth and stir-fry for another 2 to 3 minutes.

Add the fried fish to the wok and stir-fry gently, just enough to coat it with the sauce, and serve.

Sweet and Sour Stir-Fry

Pad Priew Wan

Like several Thai dishes, pad priew wan is influenced by Chinese food—but thanks to the kick from the chili paste, this is not your typical sweet and sour dish. It's not too spicy, though, and you can omit the spice altogether to make this a family-friendly favorite.

Prep time: 35 minutes

Cook time: 7 minutes

Serves: 2 to 3

2 tablespoons coconut oil

1/2 pound chicken breast, beef, or pork, chopped (about 1 cup)

1/2 cup diced red bell pepper

1/2 cup diced green bell pepper

1/2 cup diced white onion

1/2 cup chopped pineapple

1/4 cup chopped cucumber

2 teaspoons coconut aminos

2 teaspoons raw organic honey

1/4 teaspoon black pepper

1 tablespoon coconut vinegar or white vinegar

2 tablespoons tomato paste

1 1/2 teaspoons Nam Prik Pao (Thai Chili Paste, page 64)

Sea salt

Heat the oil in a wok over medium-high heat.

Add the meat and stir-fry for 3 to 4 minutes.

Add the bell peppers, onion, pineapple, and cucumber and stir-fry for another minute.

Add the coconut aminos, honey, black pepper, vinegar, tomato paste, and chili paste.

Mix together and let cook for a minute, until bubbling. Add salt to taste, adjust the other seasonings as desired, and serve.

Stir-Fried Crispy Pork Belly

Moo Krob Kua Klau

I don't know if I've ever eaten anything as good as this dish; I will never get sick of preparing it. However, be forewarned: making this dish is kind of like setting off fireworks in your kitchen, so warn the dogs and children to stand clear! Deep-frying pork belly in hot oil equals plenty of splatter, mess, and hot oil flying around, so cover your wok with a splatter guard—this is absolute must for safety, and it will keep you from having to run away fast from your deep-fried pork belly goodness! Thank you, Ninja, for your amazing skills and for teaching me how to make my favorite dish from Enjoy Bistro in Bangkok.

Prep time: 40 minutes

Cook time: 50 minutes

Serves: 3 to 4

1 pound pork belly, cut into strips 2 inches wide and 4 to 6 inches long

1 tablespoon sea salt

2 tablespoons white or coconut vinegar

2 to 3 cups palm shortening or leaf lard

1/4 cup roasted cashews, chopped

2 tablespoons coconut oil

1/2 cup red bell pepper, cut into small strips

1/2 cup green bell pepper, cut into small strips

1/2 cup yellow bell pepper, cut into small strips

1/2 small white onion, chopped

1 clove garlic, smashed with side of knife and then minced

3 medium red Thai chiles, smashed with side of knife and then sliced lengthwise

2 green onions, cut into 1-inch pieces

1 tablespoon Oyster Sauce (page 58)

1 tablespoon Sweet and Sour Sauce (page 60)

1 teaspoon maple syrup

1 tablespoon Nam Prik Pao (Thai Chili Paste, page 64)

1 tablespoon coconut aminos

Bring a large pot of water to a boil. Add the strips of pork belly and gently boil for 30 minutes, or until all the pink is gone from the pork belly.

Rinse the boiled pork belly under cold water and dry thoroughly with paper towels.

Use a fork to poke several holes in the skin of the pork belly pieces. Rub the sea salt into the skin of the pork belly. Next, massage the vinegar into the salted skin. Set the pork belly aside.

Melt the shortening in a wok or deep soup pot over high heat and heat until extremely hot.

Add the pork belly carefully to the hot oil and cover with a splatter guard. The splattering will be very dramatic at first and then begin to slow down.

Cook the pork belly, turning periodically, for about 7 to 10 minutes, until its skin is crispy and browned all over. Remove the pork belly from the hot oil and drain.

When it's cool enough to handle, slice the fried pork belly into 1/4-inch pieces and set aside.

If you are roasting your own cashews, place the cashews in dry skillet over medium to medium-high heat and stir or shake gently for about 3 to 4 minutes, until the cashews are browned. Remove from heat and set aside.

In another wok, heat the coconut oil over medium-high heat. Add the bell pepper, onion, and garlic and stir-fry for a few seconds.

Add the sliced pork, chiles, green onions, cashews, oyster sauce, sweet and sour sauce, maple syrup, chili paste, and coconut aminos. Stir-fry together for 1 minute and serve.

Stir-Fried Pork with Curry

Kua Gling Moo

Crispy, crumbly, spicy, fragrant, delicious. This dish reminds me of a typical diner breakfast special of scrambled eggs and ground beef known as Joe's Special, but without the eggs and with more flavor and spice. Serve this with Cauliflower Rice (page 40) or Sticky Rice (page 38) and Nam Pla Prik (Fish Sauce with Chiles, page 62) and prepare to be impressed with the simple yet complex flavors of this southern Thai favorite.

Prep time: 20 minutes

Cook time: 8 minutes

Serves: 2 to 3

2 tablespoons coconut or palm oil

1/2 teaspoon shrimp paste (omit if the Red Curry paste includes shrimp paste)

1 tablespoon Red Curry Paste (page 55)

3/4 pound ground pork

1/4 cup thinly sliced 1-inch pieces galangal

1 to 3 medium red Thai chiles, thinly sliced

1 tablespoon fresh green peppercorns, or black pepper to taste

1 teaspoon maple syrup

2 teaspoons water, divided

1 teaspoon turmeric powder

1/2 teaspoon fish sauce

1 tablespoon chiffonaded kaffir lime leaves

Add the oil to a hot wok over medium-high heat and mix in the shrimp paste and red curry paste. Stir constantly for about 30 seconds, until bubbling.

Add the ground pork and mix it with the paste. Cook for about 5 minutes, or until the meat is browned. Add the galangal, chiles, peppercorns, maple syrup, 1 teaspoon of the water, the turmeric powder, and the fish sauce. Cook for 1 to 2 minutes.

Add the kaffir lime leaves and the remaining teaspoon of water. Mix and serve immediately with Cauliflower Rice (page 40).

Cashew Nut Stir-Fry

A Chinese-inspired dish, this basic stir-fry is a Thai staple. Feel free to adjust the amount of chiles according to your heat tolerance, or omit the dried chiles entirely to make this a very mild meal. Pud met ma-muang is great to serve at your Thai dinner party as an option for guests who cannot take the heat!

Pud Met Ma-muang

Prep time: 30 minutes
Cook time: 8 minutes
Serves: 2 to 3

3 tablespoons coconut or palm oil

1 cup chopped chicken breast, or 10 small shrimp, shelled and deveined

1 small carrot, sliced

1/2 cup diced white onion

1 tablespoon coconut aminos

2 tablespoons Oyster Sauce (page 58)

1/2 teaspoon Nam Prik Pao (Thai Chili Paste, page 64)

1/2 teaspoon black pepper

1/2 cup roasted cashews

1 green onion, sliced into 1-inch pieces

1 teaspoon dried red chili flakes (optional)

4 small dried chiles (optional)

Sea salt

In a hot wok, heat the oil over medium-high heat. Add the chicken and stir-fry for 3 to 4 minutes. Add the carrots and white onion.

Add the coconut aminos, oyster sauce, chili paste, and black pepper and stir-fry for 1 to 2 minutes.

Add the cashews, green onion, dried red chili flakes, and small dried chiles. Salt to taste, stir, and serve.

If you decide to use shrimp instead of chicken, stir-fry the carrots and white onion first in the hot oil for a few minutes until they start to become tender, then add the shrimp, coconut aminos, oyster sauce, chili paste, black pepper, and dried red chili flakes. Sauté for another 2 to 3 minutes, just until the shrimp are pink and firm. Add the cashews, green onions, and dried whole chiles. Salt to taste and serve.

Shrimp Stir-Fry with Curry

Kung Pat Pet Sator

Here's a version of the classic southern curry stir-fry with shrimp. The first time I ate this dish I was introduced to the infamous stink beans that are so common in southern Thai cooking. Although I was grateful for the experience of having such an unusual ingredient in a traditional Thai dish, I must admit that I prefer making this dish at home with green beans.

Prep time: 20 minutes

Cook time: 6 minutes

Serves: 2 to 3

1 to 2 tablespoons coconut or palm oil

1 tablespoon Red Curry Paste (page 55)

1/4 to 1/2 teaspoon shrimp paste (omit if the red curry paste includes shrimp paste)

15 small shrimp

1 tablespoon kaffir lime leaves, chiffonaded

1/2 cup stink beans, green beans, or other veggie of your choice, or 2 cups kale or bok choy

1/2 teaspoon maple syrup

1/4 cup water

1/4 teaspoon fish sauce (optional)

Heat the oil in a wok over medium heat for about 1 minute, or until very hot.

Add the curry paste and shrimp paste to the hot oil and stir for about 15 seconds, or until sizzling.

Add the shrimp, kaffir lime leaves, stink beans, maple syrup, water, and fish sauce.

Stir-fry together for another minute or two, until the shrimp are pink and firm. Serve with Cauliflower Rice (page 40) or Jasmine Rice (page 36).

Stir-Fried Chili Shrimp

This dish, which I ate at Sandy Bay Bungalows on the island of Koh Phanagan, was one of our favorites. I was even more impressed to discover how easily it comes together at home, and this dish is now a staple for our family.

Pad Prik Kung

Prep time: 20 minutes

Cook time: 4 to 5 minutes

Serves: 2 to 3

3 tablespoons coconut or palm oil

5 to 6 medium prawns, shelled and deveined

1 clove garlic, minced

1/2 cup chopped white onion

1/4 cup chicken stock or water

1 tablespoon Oyster Sauce (page 58)

1 teaspoon coconut aminos

1 teaspoon Garlic-Infused Vinegar (page 42)

1/2 teaspoon maple syrup

1 small red Thai chile, sliced lengthwise

1 small green Thai chile, sliced lengthwise

1 green onion, cut into 1-inch slices

Sea salt and black pepper

Dash of lime juice

Heat the oil in a wok over medium-high heat.

Add the prawns and stir-fry for about 10 seconds.

Add the garlic, onion, and chicken stock and cook for another 30 seconds.

Add the oyster sauce, coconut aminos, vinegar, maple syrup, chiles, and green onion.

Stir together and simmer to reduce the sauce for 1 to 2 minutes. Stir, season to taste with sea salt, pepper, and lime juice, and serve.

Chicken Fried with Curry

I ate this simple and delicious dish at Sandy Bay Bungalows fresh out of the wok, and it was beyond good. This is another southern dish and must be served with Cauliflower Rice (page 40) or Jasmine Rice (page 36).

Pad Ped Gai

Prep time: 10 minutes

Cook time: 5 to 6 minutes

Serves: 2 to 3

1 tablespoons coconut oil, palm oil, or leaf lard

1/2 to 1 tablespoon Yellow Curry Paste (page 55)

1 to 2 tablespoons chicken broth or water

1/2 pound chicken breast, chopped (about 1 cup)

1/2 to 1 teaspoon maple syrup

Pinch of black pepper

1 tablespoon Coconut Milk (page 32)

5 sweet Thai basil leaves

1 tablespoon chiffonaded kaffir lime leaves

1 small red Thai chile, sliced in half lengthwise

Sea salt

Heat the oil in a wok over medium-high heat.

Add the curry paste and stir into the hot oil for about 15 seconds, until sizzling.

Add the chicken broth and simmer for another 30 seconds.

Add the chicken breast, maple syrup, and pepper, and stir-fry for 4 to 5 minutes, until the chicken pieces are tender and done all the way through.

Add the coconut milk, basil, kaffir lime leaves, and chile, and salt to taste. Stir-fry for 30 seconds and serve.

Stir-Fried Morning Glory

Pad Pak Bung
Fai Daeng

Morning glory is a beautiful ingredient that can often be found at your local Asian market, which is likely to carry the Chinese variety of morning glory called ong choi. *There is also a Thai variety of morning glory called* pak bung thai, *but even if Chinese morning glory is used, the Thai name of the dish always refers to "pak bung."*

Although morning glory is not always the easiest ingredient to find, if you do happen to come across some at your local Asian market or farmers market, I highly recommend making this dish. If you can't find it, I have also made this recipe with broccolini, spinach, and chard, and all have turned out absolutely wonderful. This is a great companion dish to your Thai feast, and it's extremely nutritious and very easy to make to boot!

Prep time: 15 minutes

Cook time: 6 minutes

Serves: 2 to 3

2 to 5 small red Thai chiles

5 to 6 cloves garlic

2 tablespoons coconut or palm oil

1 pound morning glory or other greens, such as broccolini, kale, spinach, or chard

1 teaspoon maple syrup

1/4 teaspoon black pepper

1 tablespoon Oyster Sauce (page 58)

1 teaspoon coconut aminos

Sea salt

White sesame seeds, for garnish (optional)

Using a wooden mortar and pestle, mash together the chiles and garlic to make a paste.

Heat the oil in a wok over high heat. Add the mashed chiles and garlic and stir-fry for about 30 seconds.

Add the morning glory, maple syrup, black pepper, oyster sauce, and coconut aminos. Add salt to taste and stir-fry for 3 to 5 minutes.

Garnish with white sesame seeds, if desired, and serve immediately.

Stir-Fried Pak Miang

Pak Miang Pad Kai

When Bow made this for me at A.O Seafood, it immediately reminded me of my favorite breakfast, sautéed spinach and eggs. Pak miang is a large leafy vegetable that is often used in stir-fry (and also to make the Leaf Bites found on page 78). Spinach is the easiest substitute for pak miang, but if you find it in your local Asian market or farmers market, you must take the opportunity to try it with this authentic recipe. Pak miang pad kai is a comforting dish that can be served alongside other Thai dishes for a dinner feast, or it can be made quickly for breakfast as a nutritious and delicious way to start your day.

Prep time: 10 minutes
Cook time: 3 to 4 minutes
Serves: 2 to 3

1/4 cup palm shortening or leaf lard

5 to 6 cloves garlic, roughly chopped

2 eggs

5 cups pak miang leaves or baby spinach leaves

4 teaspoons Oyster Sauce (page 58)

2 tablespoons chicken broth

1/4 teaspoon maple syrup (optional)

Sea salt

Melt the shortening in a wok over medium-high heat.

Add the garlic to the hot oil and sauté for about 15 seconds, just until fragrant.

Break the eggs into the hot oil and garlic and break the yolks with a spatula.

Add the pak miang leaves, oyster sauce, chicken broth, and maple syrup. Cook for 1 to 2 minutes, just until the leaves are wilted and the eggs are cooked through.

Salt to taste and serve.

Stir-Fried Mixed Vegetables

Pad Pak Ruim

Every great Thai meal needs an awesome vegetable dish, and pad pak ruim meets that need. While I was staying at Sandy Bay Bungalows, the chef there made this almost every day, and I loved the freshness of the vegetables combined with the tasty oyster sauce base.

Prep time: 15 minutes

Cook time: 5 minutes

Serves: 2 to 3

2 tablespoons coconut or palm oil

1 clove garlic, minced

1/4 cup sliced carrots

1/2 cup broccoli florets

1 cup shredded napa or green cabbage

1/4 cup sliced straw or crimini mushrooms

1 cup diced bok choy or kale leaves

1/4 cup chicken broth

1 tablespoon Oyster Sauce (page 58)

1/2 teaspoon coconut aminos

Black pepper

Heat the oil in a wok over medium-high heat.

Add the garlic, carrots, and broccoli and stir-fry for 1 to 2 minutes.

Add the cabbage, mushrooms, bok choy, chicken broth, oyster sauce, and coconut aminos and stir-fry for another 2 to 3 minutes. Add black pepper to taste and serve.

Deep-Fried Pork with Pepper and Garlic

Kao Laad Moo Thort

I learned how to make this recipe with pork, but it also works well with chicken or beef. This was my favorite street food in Thailand—it's so delicious and filling! I'm grateful that Chef Jim at Baan Pong showed me how to make this easy and flavorful dish so I can re-create my street cart favorite at home.

Prep time: 15 minutes (+ 30 minutes to marinate)

Cook time: 5 minutes

Serves: 2 to 3

1 tablespoon Oyster Sauce (page 58)

1 tablespoon coconut aminos

1/2 teaspoon finely ground black pepper

1/4 pound pork loin or meat of your choice, thinly sliced (about 1 cup)

1 cup palm shortening or leaf lard

1 egg, fried (optional)

Gratiam Jiaow (Deep-Fried Garlic, page 52; optional)

In a small bowl, stir together the oyster sauce, coconut aminos, and black pepper.

Add the thinly sliced pork to the oyster sauce mixture and stir to coat.

Cover and let marinate in the refrigerator for at least 30 minutes (overnight is even better but not necessary).

Melt the shortening in a wok over medium-high to high heat.

Once the oil is very hot, add the marinated pork. Stirring often, fry for 1 to 2 minutes, until the pork is crispy and cooked through.

Serve with a scoop of Cauliflower Rice (page 40) or Sticky Rice (page 38) topped with a fried egg and sprinkle of Gratiam Jiaow (Deep-Fried Garlic, page 52).

Try adding Chile Oil (page 50), Nam Pla Prik (Fish Sauce with Chiles, page 62), or Sweet Chili Sauce (page 72) to liven up this dish!

Indian Curry

This dish is similar to an Indian yellow curry, but the oyster sauce and heat from the Thai chiles lend it a distinctive Thai flavor. I made this dish with Chef Jim at Baan Pong and enjoy it at home as a protein-packed lunch or quick dinner for the family. Make sure you serve this with Cauliflower Rice (page 40) or Jasmine Rice (page 36).

Kao Laad Pud Pong Galii

Prep time: 30 minutes

Cook time: 10 minutes

Serves: 2 to 3

1 egg

1 teaspoon curry powder

2 tablespoons Coconut Milk (page 32)

1 teaspoon coconut aminos

1 teaspoon Oyster Sauce (page 58)

1/2 teaspoon black pepper

2 tablespoons coconut or palm oil

1 cup thinly sliced and chopped chicken, beef, or pork

1/2 white onion, chopped

1 small red Thai chile, halved

2 green onions, cut into 1-inch pieces

1/4 cup celery leaves or diced celery

Sea salt

In a small bowl, whisk together the egg, curry powder, coconut milk, coconut aminos, oyster sauce, and black pepper.

Heat the oil in a wok over high heat.

Add the meat and stir-fry for 1 to 2 minutes.

Add the egg mixture to the wok and slowly stir, coating the meat in the eggs as they cook.

Add the white onion and chile and continue to stir-fry for another few seconds.

Add the green onions and celery leaves, stir-fry for 1 to 2 minutes, and season to taste with sea salt.

Serve immediately.

Deep-Fried Fish with Chu Chee Curry Sauce

Chu Chee Pla

This is one of my favorite recipes that I learned from Pom while visiting her beautiful Cooking@home Thai Culinary School outside of Chiang Mai. During my class with Pom, it was immediately apparent that she cooks with a passion possessed only by those who truly enjoy food, and that passion comes through in this dish. The crunch of the deep-fried fish paired with the slightly spicy and slightly sweet curry sauce is divine.

Prep time: 20 minutes

Cook time: 10 minutes

Serves: 2 to 3

1/2 to 1 pound fish fillets, such as tilapia, salmon, or red snapper, deboned

1 cup palm shortening or leaf lard

Chu Chee Curry Sauce

1 1/4 cup Coconut Milk (page 32)

1 tablespoon Red Curry Paste (page 55)

2 kaffir lime leaves, torn into quarters

1/2 teaspoon sea salt

1/2 teaspoon fish sauce

2 teaspoons maple syrup

1 large red Thai chile, cut in half lengthwise, seeded, and sliced into thin strips

Sweet Thai basil leaves, for garnish

Cut the fish fillets in half and pat dry with a paper towel.

Melt the shortening in a wok over medium-high to high heat and heat until very hot.

Once the oil is hot enough to sizzle when the fish is dropped in, gently slip in the fish fillets and fry for 4 to 5 minutes or until golden brown on both sides, turning often.

Remove the fillets from the oil and set aside to drain.

To make the curry sauce: In a saucepan over medium-high heat, bring the coconut milk to a boil.

Add the curry paste and stir until blended.

Add the kaffir lime leaves and boil for 2 to 3 minutes, until fragrant and the coconut milk turns a darker red.

Add the salt, fish sauce, maple syrup, and chile and whisk together. Taste and adjust the seasoning as desired.

Drizzle the sauce over the deep-fried fish and garnish with sweet Thai basil leaves.

Deep-Fried Fish Cakes

Thod Mun Pla

I love this recipe; it's just plain good. It's important to use a mild white fish in order to let the red curry and fresh herbs shine through. When made properly, the fish cakes should be crunchy on the outside and tender, moist, and flavorful on the inside. Be sure to remove them from the oil as soon as they are golden brown and do not overcook. Have fun with this one, and of course, enjoy!

Prep time: 30 minutes

Cook time: 7 minutes

Serves: 2 to 3

1 pound white fish, finely chopped

5 kaffir lime leaves or basil leaves, chiffonaded

1/2 to 1 tablespoon Red Curry Paste (page 55)

1 teaspoon fish sauce

1 teaspoon maple syrup

1 tablespoon tapioca starch

1/4 cup finely chopped green beans

1 egg

1 to 2 cups palm shortening or leaf lard

In a medium mixing bowl, combine all the ingredients except the shortening.

Make small, palm-sized, 1/2-inch-thick patties out of the fish mixture.

Melt the shortening in a wok over high heat and heat until very hot.

Gently slide the fish cakes into the hot oil two at a time and fry, turning occasionally, for 3 to 5 minutes, until golden brown and crispy on each side.

Serve with Sweet Chili Sauce (page 72) and Sticky Rice (page 38) if desired.

Steamed Fish with Lime and Chili Sauce

Pla Nueng Ma-Nao

This fish dish is so delicate and wonderful. Use the freshest fish you can find, and try a whole fish, rather than fillets, to really get the true flavor of this authentic dish. I made this dish while staying at Samui Beach Village on the beautiful island of Koh Samui. My teacher for the day was the resort chef, Chef Eak, and this is one of his masterpieces. I know you will enjoy it!

Prep time: 30 minutes

Cook time: 30 minutes

Serves: 2 to 3 minutes

1/2 to 1 pound mild fish fillet, or 1 whole small fish (cleaned)

Sea salt

8 to 10 cilantro stems and leaves

4 to 5 kaffir lime leaves, stemmed and torn into quarters

5 to 6 thinly sliced pieces galangal

Lime and Chile Sauce

4 to 5 cloves garlic

2 to 3 small red Thai chiles

2 tablespoons minced cilantro leaves and stems

3 tablespoons lime juice

1 to 2 teaspoons fish sauce

1/2 teaspoon maple syrup (optional)

1/4 cup chicken broth

Mint leaves, for garnish

Lay the cleaned fish on a piece of foil.

Sprinkle the fish with sea salt and stuff it with the cilantro, kaffir lime leaves, and galangal, or lay these on top of the fish fillet.

Wrap the fish with foil and place it in a steamer basket. Steam for 6 to 15 minutes, depending on the size of the fillet or fish. The fish will be done when it easily flakes apart but is still moist.

To prepare the sauce: Using a wooden mortar and pestle, pound the garlic and chiles together into a paste.

In a small saucepan, heat the garlic and chile mixture, cilantro, lime juice, fish sauce, maple syrup, and chicken broth until simmering. Simmer for 4 to 5 minutes. Taste and adjust seasoning as desired.

Pour the sauce over the steamed fish, garnish with mint leaves, and serve.

Deep-Fried Fish with Thai Herbs

Pla Tot Samun Prai

This recipe is genius. Deep-frying the herbs and fish and then drenching it all in a rich, sweet, and savory sauce is more than a good idea; it's a culinary dream come true. The deep-fried herbs brighten the flavors, and the cashews add a buttery taste and crunch that create true scrumptiousness.

Prep time: 35 minutes

Cook time: 20 minutes

Serves: 2 to 3

1/2 pound fish fillet, such as snapper, cod, or salmon

Sea salt

1 to 2 cups coconut or palm oil

1 tablespoon thinly sliced lemongrass

1 tablespoon chiffonaded kaffir lime leaves

2 tablespoons basil leaves, torn into small pieces

1 tablespoon julienned galangal

1/4 cup cashews, roughly chopped

Sauce

1 tablespoon coconut or palm oil

2 tablespoons Oyster Sauce (page 58)

2 tablespoons coconut aminos

1 to 2 teaspoons maple syrup

1/2 teaspoon black pepper

Cut the fish fillet into 4-inch pieces.

Heat the oil in a wok over high heat. Once the oil is hot, add the fillets and deep-fry for 4 to 5 minutes, until golden brown on all sides.

Remove the fish from the oil and set aside to drain. Add the lemongrass, kaffir lime leaves, basil leaves, galangal, and cashews to the hot oil and deep-fry for a minute or two, until the basil leaves are crispy. Remove with a deep-fry skimmer or slotted spoon and place on top of the fried fish.

In a small saucepan, combine the sauce ingredients and heat over medium-high heat, stirring occasionally, until simmering. Pour some of the sauce over the fish and serve.

Reserve any of the remaining sauce to add to taste and serve on the side.

Fish with Tri-Flavored Sauce

Pla Sam Rot

Cooking with Chef Eak was a true experience while staying at the Samui Beach Villas on Koh Samui. Chef Eak has amazing skills, and they're apparent in his ease in the kitchen. I love the preparation of this fish: the freshness of the herbs and the tartness of the lime pair beautifully with the delicate fish.

Prep time: 30 minutes

Cook time: 20 minutes

Serves: 2 to 3

1 cup palm shortening or leaf lard

1/2 to 1 pound fish fillet, such as red snapper or cod, cut into pieces 4 to 5 inches long

Sauce

1 tablespoon coconut or palm oil

1/4 cup chopped green bell pepper

1/4 cup chopped red bell pepper

1/4 cup chopped white onion

5 cloves garlic, minced

1 to 2 teaspoons dried red chili flakes

3 tablespoons lime juice

1 to 2 teaspoons fish sauce

1/4 cup orange juice

1/4 cup chicken broth

1 teaspoon honey

Sea salt

1/4 cup chopped cilantro, plus more for garnish

Heat the shortening in a wok over high heat. Once it's melted and very hot, add the fish and deep-fry for 4 to 5 minutes, until golden brown on all sides. Remove the fish and set aside to drain.

To make the sauce: In another wok, sauté pan, or skillet, heat the coconut oil over medium-high heat.

Add the bell peppers, onion, and garlic and stir-fry for 5 to 6 minutes, until the onions are translucent.

Add the dried red chili flakes, lime juice, fish sauce, orange juice, chicken broth, and honey and bring to simmer. Add salt to taste.

Continue to simmer, stirring occasionally, for about 5 minutes to let the sauce reduce.

Add the cilantro, stir, and pour the sauce over the fried fish.

Garnish with fresh cilantro and serve immediately.

Desserts

Pumpkin Custard

I love this dessert, which is made with delicious coconut milk and eggs and cooked in a hollowed-out Thai pumpkin. It's about as nutritious as dessert can get, and it's not too sweet. I made this while cooking with Pom at her culinary school, and she used a Thai pumpkin called fuk tong that had the most amazing sweet flavor. A small heirloom squash, like a kabocha, would be a wonderful replacement for the fuk tong.

Sankaya Phak Tong

Prep time: 20 minutes

Cook time: 45 to 60 minutes

Serves: 3 to 4

4 eggs

1 cup Coconut Milk (page 32)

1/4 cup honey or maple syrup

1/2 teaspoon sea salt

1/2 teaspoon vanilla extract

1- to 2-pound small fuk tong (Thai pumpkin), kabocha squash, or sugar pumpkin

1/4 fuk tong, kabocha squash, or sugar pumpkin, cut into pieces 1/4 inch thick and 2 inches long (1/2 cup)

In a small bowl, whisk together the eggs, coconut milk, honey, sea salt, and vanilla.

Strain the mixture through a sieve and discard anything that is left behind in the sieve.

Cut the top off the pumpkin and remove the seeds.

Peel and thinly slice another 1/4 of a pumpkin or enough for 1/2 cup.

Pour the egg mixture into the hollowed-out pumpkin until it reaches 1/4 inch from the top and sprinkle in the pumpkin slices.

Use a stacked steamer or an extra-large soup pot and vegetable steamer to steam the pumpkin for 45 minutes to an hour, or until the custard is set all the way through and the pumpkin is soft. The custard is done when a knife inserted in the middle comes out clean. To keep the pumpkin from cracking, make sure that the heat is not too high during steaming. You can also place the pumpkin in a bowl to help it hold together while cooking.

Let the custard and the pumpkin cool completely in the refrigerator.

Cut the cooled pumpkin with the custard into slices, as pictured, to serve.

Crispy Fried Bananas

Kluay Khaek

Bananas, bananas everywhere! That's what you see at a typical Thai market. There are over 100 different varieties of bananas grown in Thailand, and let me tell you, they are not at all like the bananas commonly found here in the States. The bananas used for kluay khaek are typically the shorter, wider bananas known as "Burro bananas." You can sometimes find this variety in major grocery stores and in Asian or Hispanic markets. Starchier and more plantain-like but still sweet, Burro bananas are great for frying. You can also make this dish with standard bananas; just make sure they are not too ripe. But to get the real taste of Thai street food, try to find a more exotic banana when you make this dish.

Prep time: 10 minutes

Cook time: 5 to 6 minutes

Serves: 4 to 5

Batter

1 cup tapioca flour

1/4 cup sparkling water

2 eggs

1/4 cup finely shredded coconut

2 teaspoons white sesame seeds

1 teaspoon whole cane sugar (optional)

4 to 5 Burro bananas or other banana of your choice

1 to 2 cups palm shortening or leaf lard

In a medium bowl, whisk together the batter ingredients and set aside.

Peel the bananas and cut into 3-inch pieces.

Melt the shortening in a wok over high heat and heat until very hot.

Drop the bananas into the batter and coat them well.

Drop the battered banana pieces 2 to 3 at a time into the hot oil and deep-fry, turning occasionally, for 3 to 4 minutes, or until golden brown on all sides.

Serve immediately!

If you have any leftover batter, drop spoonfuls into the hot oil to make little deep-fried balls of deliciousness.

Thai Coconut Pancakes

Khanom Bahbin

These little Thai pancakes are truly a special treat. I was able to make them grain-free and just as delicious as the original by substituting a mixture of arrowroot and coconut flour for the rice flour, and the coconut flour adds just a little bit to the existing coconut taste. You can also make them the traditional way, with rice flour; I've provided instructions for both options. Thai pancakes are typically served plain, but they're also delicious topped with sliced bananas or slathered with butter. These are quick, easy to make, and absolutely delightful—I love to make them as a weekend morning treat for my family. Thank you, Pom, for showing me how to make khanom bahbin.

Prep time: 15 minutes

Cook time: 10 minutes

Yield: 12 to 14 small pancakes

Traditional Khanom Bahbin

2 cups Coconut Milk (page 32)

2 tablespoons whole cane sugar or maple syrup

1/4 teaspoon sea salt

1 cup sticky rice flour

1/2 cup rice flour

2 tablespoons shredded unsweetened coconut

1 teaspoon black sesame seeds

1 teaspoon white sesame seeds

½ tablespoon coconut oil

In a medium mixing bowl, combine the coconut milk, sugar, and salt, and stir until the sugar and salt are dissolved.

Gradually add the sticky rice flour and then the regular rice flour a little at the time and stir until you have a smooth batter.

Add the shredded coconut and black and white sesame seeds and mix well.

Heat a frying pan, flat-bottomed wok, or crêpe pan over low to medium heat, for 1 to 2 minutes, or until it is very hot. Add the coconut oil, then spoon 2 tablespoons of batter into the pan and cook for 3 to 4 minutes, until is the pancake is firm and golden. Flip and cook the other side until golden brown and firm.

Serve immediately.

Grain-Free Khanom Bahbin

1/4 cup arrowroot flour

1/4 cup coconut flour

2 tablespoons finely shredded coconut

1 teaspoon black sesame seeds

1 teaspoon white sesame seeds

1/4 teaspoon sea salt

1/2 cup Coconut Milk (page 32)

3 eggs

2 tablespoons maple syrup

1 tablespoon coconut oil or butter (or more as needed to fry the pancakes)

In a small mixing bowl, combine the arrowroot flour, coconut flour, shredded coconut, black and white sesame seeds, and sea salt.

In another small bowl, whisk together the coconut milk, eggs, and maple syrup.

Stir the coconut milk mixture into the dry ingredients and whisk until smooth.

Heat the coconut oil in a skillet over medium heat. Drop in about 2 to 3 tablespoons of batter per pancake.

Once the edges start to look done, flip the pancakes and cook for 1 to 2 minutes on the other side. Add more coconut oil to the pan as needed.

Serve immediately.

Mango Sticky Rice

Khao Niaow Ma Muang

This beloved Thai dessert is decadent, sweet, salty, and just too good. For those of you who do not eat rice, I've found that using coconut flakes creates a consistency similar to the traditional sticky rice. The texture will not be exactly like rice, but the flavor is spot-on and the result is just as delicious as the authentic rice version. I have provided recipes for both the authentic sticky rice version and the coconut version without rice. Chef Ninja was the first person to introduce me to the yumminess that is mango sticky rice, and I hope you enjoy this decadent dessert!

Prep time: 10 minutes

Cook time: 5 to 7 minutes

Serves: 2 to 3

Traditional Sticky Rice

1/2 cup Coconut Milk (page 32)

2 tablespoons honey

1 teaspoon vanilla extract

Pinch of sea salt

1 cup warm Sticky Rice (page 38)

Coconut "Sticky Rice"

1 cup finely shredded coconut flakes

1 cup Coconut Milk (page 32)

1 tablespoon honey

1/2 teaspoon sea salt

1/4 teaspoon vanilla extract

1 ripe mango, sliced

Sauce (optional)

1/2 cup Coconut Milk (page 32) (if you don't make your own, make sure you use the full-fat kind)

1 tablespoon honey

1/8 teaspoon salt

If you are using traditional sticky rice, mix the coconut milk, honey, vanilla, and sea salt in a small saucepan and heat over medium-high heat, stirring constantly, until the milk starts to simmer. Pour the hot milk over the cooked sticky rice and mix together.

If you decide not to use sticky rice, combine the coconut flakes, coconut milk, honey, salt, and vanilla in a small saucepan and bring to a simmer over medium-high heat. Let the mixture simmer, stirring occasionally, until it becomes thick.

Top with the sliced mango.

To make the sauce: In a small saucepan, bring the coconut milk and honey to a simmer. Stir constantly for about 4 to 5 minutes, until the sauce begins to reduce and thicken. Drizzle over the mango and sticky rice (or "sticky rice") and serve.

Bananas in Coconut Milk

Gluoy Bwod Chee

This is a staple Thai dessert, and I cooked, ordered, and ate this dish all over the country. Nusi, the owner of a cooking school in Bangkok, introduced it to me during my first few days in Thailand, and I fell in love with this easy-to-make dish that highlights the sweet saltiness found in all Thai treats. The sweetness can be easily adjusted to your liking; you can even omit the honey or maple syrup altogether and just enjoy the natural sweetness of the coconut milk with the ripe banana.

Prep time: 5 minutes
Cook time: 10 minutes
Serves: 2 to 3

1/2 cup Coconut Milk (page 32)
1 cup water
1/4 teaspoon sea salt
1/2 tablespoon vanilla extract
2 tablespoons honey or maple syrup
3 ripe bananas, quartered

In a medium saucepan, combine the coconut milk and water.

Whisk in the sea salt, vanilla, and honey and bring to a simmer.

Add the banana pieces to the coconut milk mixture and gently stir. Bring back to a simmer and let the bananas cook, stirring occasionally, for 10 minutes.

Serve immediately.

Travel Log
& Tips for
Visiting Thailand

Meet the Team and Acknowledgments

John, Jaden, and Rowan Fragoso

"The boys," as I like to refer to my crew. My husband, John, and my two littlest guys—Jaden, who was 9 during our trip, and Rowan, who was 5—are my constant companions, and I wouldn't have it any other way. We are officially world travelers now, and I am amazed at the resiliency of my little family. Rowan is a homebody, and every time we leave he misses his dogs, his friends, his uncle, his big brother Coby, and his toys, and yet every time we come home from an adventure he asks when we can return! Rowan lives life to the fullest and everything he does is big, loud, and brave. He is so full of life, the one who keeps me on my toes, and I'm so glad that he is mine. Jaden keeps us all in check and on track, and he's always engrossed in what's happening. Jaden never misses a thing and is eager to try anything new, including snacking on crunchy insects and snorkeling in unknown and choppy seas, and he always shares with us his gift of music. He is always by my side, my friend, my son, and someone I already respect and look up to. Jaden's old soul has taught me so much about life and the importance of always listening to, respecting, and being attentive to the ones you love. John is my hero, my friend, my husband, and my true confidant. He loves me always, no matter what. Thank goodness for that, because often I can be a lot to live with, and without John these journeys—not to mention my life—would not be what they are.

The Lang Family

Mike, America, Giana, and Catalina. The Langs are our dear friends—more than friends, we consider them family. I'm forever grateful that the Lang family joined us on this adventure. Mike has been our food photographer for years now, and it only made sense to have him accompany us. America, Mike's wife, is like a sister to me, and I couldn't imagine Mike coming on the journey without her and their girls, Giana and Catalina. The Langs are some of the kindest, most understanding, sweetest, and all-around best people I know. Without the support of Mike and America, these books simply wouldn't happen, and our lives would be a lot less fulfilling. Mike and America, thank you both so much for working on this project for hours on end and in crazy conditions, and Mike, thank you especially for only bringing two changes of clothes on our five-week trip in order to have enough room for all of your camera gear. Giana and Catalina are two bright spots in my life. Brave and funny, sweet and patient, Giana and Cat put up with a whole lot of crazy experiences on our trip! I will never forget our first "squatty potty" adventure—I promise you both, the next place we go will have Western toilets (hopefully). Lang family, without you our adventure would have been very dull indeed, and I can't wait to see where life takes us together next.

Mayela Wickham

Mayela kept our children safe and brought us so much joy on our trip. She helped make bug sanctuaries with the kiddos, swam with them for hours, hunted down snacks, calmed tired and grumpy children, and always kept her calm, bright, happy demeanor, no matter how grueling our circumstances. Mayela was our quiet warrior, and she bravely made her way through Thailand with us without a single complaint or worry, always ready to help and happy to be there. I'm so glad to have you in our lives; you are not just a babysitter, you are a sister, a daughter, and a lifelong friend. We love you, Mayela!

Our Home Team

Coby

Thank you, sweet boy, for always supporting your mom. I cherish our talks and our time together. You have been my endless source of strength since the day you were born, with your love and courage and unyielding belief that kindness and compassion is always the answer. I am so proud of you, son, today and always. Thank you for coming home from school and diving into whatever crazy dish I cooked up during the day and giving me your honest feedback—not just on the dishes in this book, but on everything in life. Who would have thought that an eighteen-year-old would be wiser than his mom about so many things? But knowing you, I'm not at all surprised that you are.

Alexa, Joe, Drake, Mikayla, and Trevor

Voyer family, I hope you all know how much I love each of you. Alexa, when people ask what you do for Everyday Paleo, all I can say is that you are my angel. The last two book projects would never have taken flight if it weren't for your calm guidance and insight. You truly have tightened this ship like no one else could, and your perspective, dedication, support, and excitement have been nothing short of a blessing. The best thing, though? You're part of a package deal, and the Fragoso family is grateful for all of you; Alexa, Joe, Drake, Mikayla, and Trevor, you all have enriched our lives and brought us so much joy, and I know that with all of us together, the future is bright!

Dain

If I could set you up with tacos for life, I would. In fact, I think I'll look into that. Thank you for keeping Everyday Paleo going while I wander around the world doing other stuff. You are never frazzled, always there when we need you, and a true friend. I'm so grateful for you.

Mark

There is not enough gratitude on the planet to adequately cover the intense amount of work that Mark put into this project. Thank you, brother, for your dedication, patience, and love. Without you on our team we would truly be a sinking ship. There's nothing like having a brother to hold you up when you are done, remind you to rest when you are tired, and make you laugh until you want to pee your pants. I wouldn't do any of this without you; truly, I *couldn't* do any of this without you. I'm honored to have you as part of the Everyday Paleo team; you have added so much value to our lives, and we are all forever grateful.

Laura H.

Thank you, sweet Laura, for letting me hide in your house to write and for always being there for my family. Thank you for making me tea, listening to me, feeding me, and most importantly, thank you for loving me. You are truly my guardian angel. Love you.

The Entire Everyday Paleo and EPLifeFit Team

Jason, Sheryl, Rachel, Kris, Jeromie, and everyone else I know I am forgetting, you are all so valued and adored. Thank you for being such positive forces in the universe.

My Family

Dad, Sandy, Laura, Eric, and Shaela, thank you all for always loving, supporting, and encouraging me. I'm so lucky to have you as my family. Thank you also to Aunt Mary and Uncle Dean for spending two weeks with us tasting, testing, cleaning, cooking, and helping me to organize my life in order to get this book off the ground. I will never forget how much fun that time was, and your help was truly the kickstart we needed! I love you all.

Planning Our Trip to Thailand

Planning our trip through the fascinating, beautiful, and awe-inspiring country of Thailand was easy. Why? Because we didn't do a whole lot of planning. We were fortunate that several friends and even my publisher have spent a great deal of time in Thailand, and after a few phone calls and dinner conversations with our eager-to-help support network, we felt ready to do our own research and figure out where we wanted to go in order to collect the widest array of recipes and experiences.

After discussing our plans with our travel partners, the Lang family, we decided that it might be best not to make any solid or scheduled plans. We had a rough idea of the regions that we wanted to visit, but we didn't want to commit to staying in any particular place for a predetermined length of time. Thailand is known as a backpacker's destination, so we decided to explore the country from a backpacker's perspective and let our

adventures take us where they may. However, I did have some concerns about heading to unknown country without an itinerary. With nine of us traveling together, including four children under the age of ten, I knew that it could be challenging not to have every leg of our trip planned or even know where we might be sleeping. But hey, we are all pretty brave and a little bit crazy, so we jumped in with both feet (a few times on our journey, quite literally).

Thai Culture and What to Know Before You Go

It's impossible to understand what Southeast Asia is like unless you've been there. You can imagine, read books, look up articles, study Thai culture, and ask your friends who have been there—but really, I promise, you simply can't know.

What struck me the most about Thai culture is that, holy guacamole, living here in the West, we are truly spoiled with *stuff*. Too much stuff! And even though we have such an abundance of material goods, we lack a lengthy history and, since America is truly a melting pot, a national culture like those in other parts of the world. I would give up all of my stuff if it meant having roots, a history, a story passed down from generation to generation that I could hold on to and give to my own children. I am Native American, but my family did not teach me about my people. They did not tell me stories that made me feel connected to my ancestors or where I came from. Why? Because no one taught *them*, because there was shame associated with being of Native American descent during my grandmother's generation. My story is unfortunately common in America, for those of every heritage.

When you visit a country that is rich with history, you can tell almost as soon as you step off the plane that stuff is not nearly as important there as the people themselves. Food is important. Work is important. Family is important. Traditions, culture, honor, doing the right thing: these are the things that are valued and held in high regard.

The history of Thailand is complicated and a bit confusing, and the culture is very different from what we are used to in America. Predominately Buddhist, the Thai people have many beliefs, practices, and traditions that most Westerners are not used to. However, one amazing part about our travels has been the important life lessons that one can only learn from a different culture. Although we didn't make specific plans for our trip in terms of where we wanted to go, before we left we did take the time to learn about Thai culture and how to behave, dress, speak, and act without offending anyone. My goal, first and foremost, is always to honor and respect others and teach my children to do so as well, no matter where in the world we might be. The way I live my life is simply different from others', not necessarily better, and I long to learn from others in order to apply new concepts to my own philosophies and live the best life possible.

With this in mind, here's a very brief glimpse into Thai culture and what to expect if you decide to travel to this amazing country.

Culture

As I mentioned, Thailand is a Buddhist country, 95 percent of the population practicing Buddhism. This might seem like just a trivial fact, but Buddhism defines the underpinnings of Thai culture and is a main reason that Thailand's customs are vastly different than Western culture's. Most of the Thai etiquette that I'll explain later is tied directly to the fact that the population is predominantly Buddhist. Thailand is also a monarchy, and together, these facts make the country and culture very different from America.

The king is held in very high regard, and it's extremely important to always show respect for the king and the royal family. In fact, speaking negatively about the king or the royal family is against the law and punishable by three to fifteen years in prison. With this in mind, we all found it better to say nothing of the king at all, just in case whatever we said was somehow lost in translation and came across as offensive. I think we were a little more scared than we should have been about this, since we had no reason to bad-mouth the king or the royal family, but it seemed safer to just listen and smile when someone mentioned anything about the ruler of the country. We saved our daringness for other, more exciting things.

Thai culture is influenced by Indian and Chinese tradition, but most of their practices come strictly from the evolution of Thai culture. Thai people are very driven by a few distinct values, and probably the most important of these are respect, self-control, and avoiding conflict. The Thai people strive to always "save face" because they consider losing face, lying, and showing anger to be very shameful. This is, in part, why Thailand is known as the land of smiles. In Thailand, it's very important not to argue, be rude, or be loud and dramatic about what upsets you; instead, the right thing to do is save face and smile. We learned this quickly when bartering. You can still hold your own and not get taken advantage of, but the kinder you are and the more you smile while bartering, the more likely you will be to get your way. Being rude or not smiling is not respected in Thailand, so save face while there and do as the locals do: smile!

However, this does not mean that behind every smile there is kindness. As a tourist, it's very important to be careful, which is why we often avoided the most popular tourist locations and always stayed together. The same is true wherever you travel—in fact, we should have the same level of awareness even in our hometowns! The good news is, with some mindfulness and safety precautions, traveling to Thailand is very safe. I've seen more crime in my hometown of Chico, California, than in Thailand, and certainly nothing scary happened to us that we didn't deliberately choose (like snorkeling in deep, choppy water or trying to drive a scooter and learning quickly that I'm much better off as a passenger). It's important to note here that yes, human trafficking and prostitution are particular problems in Thailand and other parts of Southeast Asia, but that should not deter you from visiting. I'll touch more on that later.

The high value the Thai people place on respect shows in the way people treat their elders and families. There is a hierarchy of respect, and elders and those who are of higher social status—which is determined primarily by wealth, age, and the personal or political power of the individual— are always at the top. Children are expected to respect their parents at all times, and this holds true into adulthood. Families are very close-knit and often extended families live together in one household: aunts, uncles, grandparents, parents, and children.

The Thai people are jovial and, although not always obviously affectionate, love to have fun. Laughing and having a good time is truly the essence of life in Thailand. This important cultural element is known as *sanuk*. Sanuk embodies the playfulness and sense of humor that is often displayed by the Thai people. They love to poke fun in a playful manner and look for the humor in a conversation, and you'll often see this type of exchange between friends on the street or in your own interactions. We found out quickly that if someone does not understand you, the common response from the Thai people is laughter. It actually makes things easier, and we ended up adopting the philosophy. Whenever we were lost, frustrated, or angry, we would just laugh out loud and usually it would cheer us right up, because it's kind of funny just to laugh at nothing. *Sanuk!*

Etiquette

It's important to remove your shoes before entering certain Thai establishments. Most homes and even places of business require you to remove your shoes. How can you tell? Simply look for the piles of shoes in front of the door, and if there is an obvious place to take your shoes off before you go in, then follow suit!

Speaking of shoes, the Thai people think of the feet as the lowest part of the body. (Of course, geographically, this is correct!) They do not ever point their feet at someone or show the soles of their feet to another person; this is thought to be as bad as showing your middle finger. Also, do not touch a Thai person on the head. The head is thought to be the most sacred part of the body and should be respected.

Modest clothing is important in Thailand, especially when visiting a spiritual place like a Buddhist temple, known as a *wat*. You must see the wats while in Thailand; they are everywhere and they are beautiful, spiritual, almost mystical places. Make sure you have your shoulders covered—no tank tops—and remove your shoes before entering the temples.

Modesty in behavior is also important. Thai people do not show public displays of affection; you will not see couples holding hands or kissing in front of others. It is kind to respect this aspect of Thai culture and remember that public displays of affection are considered taboo, something to be done only in private.

The typical greeting in Thailand is called a *wai* (pronounced "way"). The wai is done by placing your hands together in a prayer position and bowing slightly. We learned that it's important to wai to everyone when you first meet them, to your elders when you greet them, and to those who have more "importance" than you do. You do not, however, have to wai to hotel staff, people who are waiting on you, or children. However, it's always polite to wai, so we tended to wai on the side of caution. To this day, John, the kids, and I still catch ourselves greeting people and saying thank you with a wai. It's actually really great to see that this greeting of respect became so ingrained in us, since most Americans (including us) don't have a formal way of showing respect, and sometimes this can be perceived as rudeness.

The Language and Thai Names

A few key Thai phrases will help you a lot in Thailand: mainly, "hello" and "where is the bathroom?" These two phrases got us a long way, believe it or not. We learned rather quickly, though, that although we thought we knew how to say these phrases correctly, when we tried them out, we were promptly laughed at and corrected. It's also tricky because the Thai language has different phrases or words depending on if the speaker is a man or a woman. Most men end their greetings with "krap" and women with "kaa." I recommend purchasing a Thai phrase book before you go, but you will learn more just by going, especially when it comes to correct pronunciation.

Interestingly, names are used differently in Thailand than in the West. Everyone is given a name at birth, of course, but they are also given a nickname. Except for formal situations, Thai people always use their nicknames. Nicknames are picked based on several factors. Parents often choose an English word that they like the sound of or a word that reminds them of how their child looks. Wondering what name we'd encounter next was one of the interesting and fun parts of our journey!

7-Elevens and Pharmacies

More than once we were saved by a 7-Eleven or a pharmacy. Both were on every street corner in every city we visited in Thailand. 7-Elevens are perfect for restocking supplies like shampoo, soap, toilet paper, cleansing wipes and tissues, snacks like sliced apples, nuts, and yogurt (if you eat dairy, of course), and clean drinking water. They're also great for asking for directions and re-upping the minutes on your cell phone. (You'll need to switch out your SIM card when you get to Thailand in order to have a Thai phone number, so you can call to make reservations or flight arrangements as you travel around the country.)

Pharmacies are also everywhere, and you can ask for anything you need without a prescription. We needed a pharmacy twice on our journey and were very grateful for their expertise. The pharmacists all seemed very knowledgeable and were very willing to help, and trust me, when you are not feeling well in a foreign country, it's nice to have a friendly face to help you. (Here's a short list of what we bought at the pharmacies we visited: Motrin, eye drops for a case of conjunctivitis, medicine to help calm horrible bug bites, and Tiger Balm for our incredibly sore muscles after walking miles and miles in hot and humid conditions.) One other thing, for female travelers: it's extremely hard to find feminine products in Thailand, so if that will be an issue during your trip, be sure to bring plenty from home.

Transportation: Planes, Trains, Scooters, Tuk-Tuks, Taxis, and Songtaos—Oh My!

Bangkok is a scary madness of motor scooters, taxis, and tuk-tuks. I would not opt to drive in Bangkok, ever, ever, ever, but if you are feeling particularly brave, go for it—just don't e-mail me to complain when you do not have the best experience. We opted for taxis in Bangkok for the most part and arranged for a van to pick us up at the airport. Try to find a taxi driver who uses his meter, and don't ride in a cab whose meter is off unless you negotiate a price prior to getting in the car. Better yet, only take metered cabs, so you can see exactly what you are being charged. Once you have an idea of what a legitimate taxi ride might cost, you can venture out into the land of tuk-tuks.

Tuk-tuks are three-wheeled motorcycles that are usually covered to provide some shade, but with the sides open to the air, be ready for some heat and exhaust inhalation. Tuk-tuks are often gussied up with lights, frills, and decorations and are quite a sight to see on the roads of Bangkok.

Tuk-tuk drivers are known for scamming tourists, so here's some tips to make sure you do not get the short end of the stick at the end of your tuk-tuk ride. *Tuk* means "cheap," but that's not always the case with these flashy rides. Tuk-tuk drivers will sometimes offer you a deal as long as they can take you to certain shops. Always say no to this! They will try to get you to buy from shops that have arrangements with the drivers, and your quick ride will turn into a day of bartering and frustration. If you decide to ride in a tuk-tuk, finding one away from the popular tourist destinations is always your best bet, and always, always negotiate a price before you get in. I recommend riding in a tuk-tuk at least once for the true Thailand experience. Tuk-tuks are made for two people, but they will cram in as many as possible, and we tested the limits on one occasion when we crammed eight of us into the back of one tuk-tuk. Not advisable, but extremely fun and memorable nonetheless.

Songtaos are found in the more rural areas, such as Chiang Mai and the islands that we visited. They are pickup trucks with covered cabs and benches installed in the bed of the truck for your riding pleasure. As with the tuk-tuks and unmetered cabs, be sure to negotiate a price before you get in. Most of all, have fun! Transportation can be scary but it's always a huge adventure, and you never know who your driver might be or what stories or adventures might result from one little ride in a tuk-tuk or taxi.

We also rented scooters in the smaller rural areas that we visited. I personally did not drive one; I tried but crashed immediately, so I let John drive as I held on in the back for dear life. If you rent a scooter, be sure to ask your hotel to recommend a rental place in order to avoid any scams (a popular one is inventing damage claims when you return the rental). Also, try to avoid areas that are congested with traffic. Thai folks drive fast, and there are not a lot of rules of the road (that are followed, anyway), so watch out for people passing on all sides and stay alert. Otherwise, riding scooters in Thailand was an absolute thrill, and I have awesome memories of cruising around small islands with John, Mike, and America towards the end of our trip, soaking in the sights and feeling free and alive.

If you decide to travel from region to region while in Thailand, I highly recommend taking commuter flights instead of trains or buses. The short flights between major cities are incredibly inexpensive and much more reliable. You can opt for the train, but with a group as large as ours and with children who really didn't want to be cooped up in a train all day, it made the most sense to take the commuter flights. I highly recommend Bangkok Air and Thai Smile Airways. Both are very professional, safe, and reliable.

Economics and Logistics

Thailand is expensive to get to but can be inexpensive once you're there. The Thai baht is their form of currency, and the exchange rate is definitely in our favor at around 31 Thai bahts to a US dollar. It's simple to live like royalty while in Thailand even on a limited budget, if you are willing to avoid the five-star resorts and seek out smaller, locally owned establishments. You can absolutely drain your bank account staying in the finer hotels and dining in the touristy districts, but with a little research and ingenuity, you can eat the best food you have ever tasted, sleep on beachfront property, and have massages like you've never experienced in your life for only a few dollars a day.

The majority of the places we stayed at cost between $20 and $75 per night, and we ate food from street vendors and small restaurants for what felt like pennies. One of our more memorable meals was at Awanahouse in Chiang Mai, where we ordered probably fourteen plates of food and paid only $40. Amazing. If you travel to Thailand, go with a backpacker's perspective, do some online research on hotels and restaurants in advance, and ask around for recommendations when you arrive. You will be pleasantly surprised at how far a little

bit of money will take you, and you'll get to enjoy the true Thai experience.

I highly recommend that you pack light for Thailand. We spent five weeks in the country, and each of us carried one backpack. That's it. We brought clothes that dried quickly and wore our clothes as many times as possible before washing them. Also, clothing is fairly inexpensive in Thailand, so we ended up buying a few more outfits once there. We also shipped home souvenirs rather than lugging them around with us for the duration of the trip. It took forever for what we sent home to arrive, but it was fun to get a big box of Thai goodies a few weeks after our return, and the wait was well worth not having to carry everything with us while traveling.

Bathrooms, Baby Wipes, and Napkins (Fun and Funny Facts!)

This is as good a time as any to mention the squatty potties that you will find in Southeast Asia. Squatting over a hole in the ground is the norm in this part of the world, but there are Western-style toilets in most hotels. This is not the case in all locations, though, and we learned quickly to be prepared for the traditional Thai bathrooms. Most local restaurants and even tourist spots like the zoo are typically equipped with the traditional squatty potty. The little girls especially were thrown off by this, but they were brave troopers, and after day one we all knew what to expect. My advice: carry baby wipes with you, because toilet paper is rarely found in Thai bathrooms (they use a hose for cleaning up after using the restroom, a practice none of us were quite willing to embrace just yet).

One place you will find plenty of toilet paper is at the table. For whatever reason, and it's a question I failed to ask, most tables are stocked with rolls of toilet paper to use as napkins. Not very effective if you ask me, but that's the norm.

Also, although Thai bathrooms sometimes had sinks, they typically had no soap, so we all carried with us a little package of wipes and hand sanitizer.

Thai Massage

Massage parlors are everywhere in Thailand. You'll find massages offered in huts on the beach, outside on the streets, and in the markets; there are literally massage parlors on almost every block in Bangkok. The traditional Thai massage includes stretching and kneading muscles and is done without lotion and while you are fully clothed. Foot massage is also very popular, and trust me, after walking the streets of Bangkok all day, you will be pleading for a foot massage. You can also ask for a standard oil massage, which is more relaxing than the therapeutic Thai massage.

The history of Thai massage is as long, convoluted, and confusing as the history of Thailand itself, but a lot of the practice comes from Chinese reflexology and is thought to have developed first as treatment for the royal Thai family. Some people who visit Thailand are frightened of getting massages or worry that the establishment will not be "professional," but it's obvious which places offer legitimate massage and which do not. We definitely took advantage of the numerous places to get massages, because where else in the world can you make this treat a daily occurrence for the same price as a large Americano at Starbucks? It's absolutely worth it. Several times on our trip the kids drifted off to sleep while having their feet massaged after long hours being led around the humid streets of Thailand.

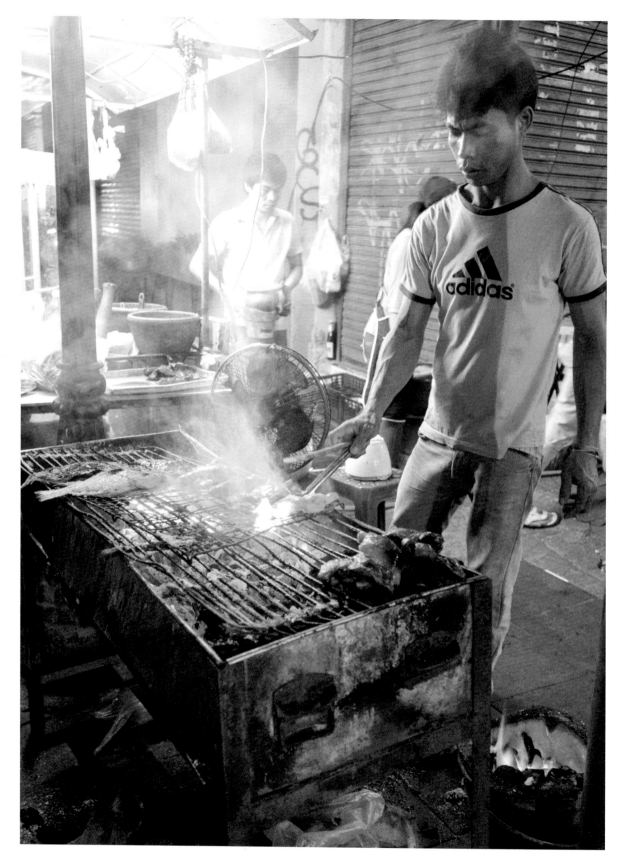

Food Culture

Food is extremely important in Thai culture. People often greet each other by saying, *"Gen khaolaewruyung?"*: "Have you had rice yet?" Thai culture is a culture of sharing, and they genuinely want to share food with you! Food is always served family style, and at restaurants, diners order a few more dishes than there are people and everyone gets their own rice and then passes around the other dishes. It's such a beautiful way to eat and be together. We teach our children at a very young age to share, and sharing nourishment is such a wonderful tradition to start with your own family.

Thai people learn to cook from whomever in their family is the best cook and recipes and methods are passed from generation to generation, so even the preparation of the food is part of sharing in a way. Unfortunately, the Thai food culture is changing due to globalization. While Thai culture is affected more by its neighbors, Japan, China, and Korea, than by Western culture, Thailand is beginning to see an inundation of fast food chains, processed food, candy, and other garbage. More and more of the staple Thai ingredients and foods, such as curry pastes and coconut milk, are now available pre-made; this is not always such a bad thing because the ingredients are often exactly the same as when they're made at home, but unfortunately some of the healthier traditions have been thrown to the wayside—the animal fats used in cooking, for instance, have now been replaced by soybean oil or highly processed palm oils.

Human Trafficking

The tough reality is that sex trafficking, child trafficking, and prostitution are severe problems in Thailand. There is great work being done to counteract these issues, but the situation is still the giant elephant in the room in many parts of Southeast Asia. The best way that you can help is by not ignoring the problem. In Thailand, "bad" things are often not discussed, and a lot of what we consider to be taboo goes unnoticed. This can be good and bad. When you're there, you get a sense of slipping away, getting lost, and being unobserved, which feels great while on vacation but which also encourages the above-mentioned problems. If you want to help, there are several organizations working hard to stop human trafficking that have made amazing headway over the years. For more information, visit www.worldvision.org and preventhumantrafficking.org.

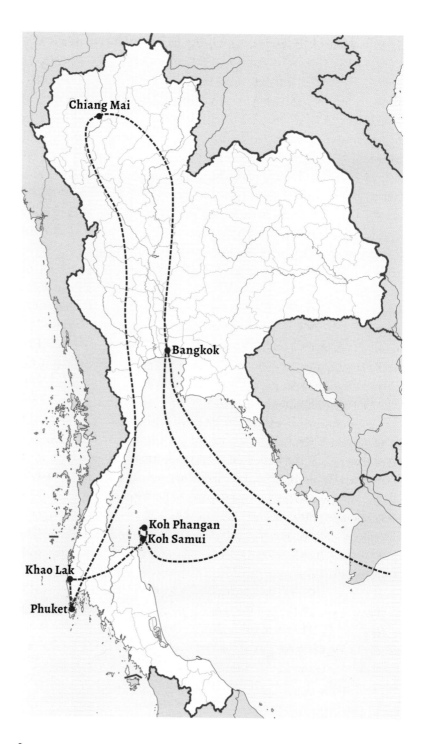

The Adventure Begins

Our flight from San Francisco to Bangkok had a layover in China. Our boys had always wanted to go to China so the little stop was exciting to them, though not so much to the rest of us, knowing how long and grueling the trip ahead would be.

I also want to visit China someday, but layovers are layovers no matter where you end up, and spending a few exhausted hours in an airport is not exactly my idea of visiting a country. However, we are all troopers, and more than anything the feeling in the air was pure excitement. As we sat on the runway in San Francisco, I let my thoughts wander to the trip ahead and erased any expectations from my mind. Although the motivation for the trip was to do research for this book, I needed something more. I needed some time away, time to be a part of something I never had been a part of before. I was longing for adventure, a change of pace, and a challenge. I wanted to enter into this journey with an open mind and no preconceptions. Southeast Asia: those words alone sounded incredibly far from home, and saying them made my wanderer spirit smile.

Sometimes leaving behind your comfort zone opens a door to magical revelations, moments of clarity, and occasionally tough learning curves that either strengthen your convictions or turn them directly on their head. That's why I was taking this trip: to learn, to grow, and to have my own stubborn thoughts on how things work be proven totally wrong. The willingness to embrace new perspectives is the best part of learning and growing; different may not always be better, but sometimes different is exactly what we need to make us just a little more aware of how big this world really is and just how much opportunity we all have to grow.

As I mulled over these convoluted thoughts, I realized that it had been over an hour and we were *still* sitting on the runway in San Francisco. We only had a two-hour layover in China before our flight to Bangkok, and the realization began to creep in that we were not going to make it. But there's not a lot one can do when stuck on a plane other than go with the flow. By the time whatever delayed our flight was resolved, it had become crystal clear that no one knew what would happen once we got to China. This little hiccup was a indication of just how spontaneous our entire trip was going to be.

Our flight was so late getting into China that we ended up having to stay our first night in Asia in Beijing rather than Bangkok. The airline put us up in a strange hotel with very hard, tiny beds, but nevertheless, the following morning we all woke up a little less disoriented than the night before and feasted on the most eclectic and crazy breakfast buffet I have ever seen. We ate several varieties of stir-fry, attempted some eggs that were not just fermented but pretty much downright rotten, sipped our coffee, and laughed at the kids, whose orange juice turned out to be a warm, weird citrus drink that none of us could quite figure out. Before we were bussed back to the airport, we said good-bye to China, knowing that the real adventure was about to begin.

We were on our way to Bangkok.

Bangkok

After a long day of travel, we walked out of the Bangkok airport and onto the street to wait for the van that I had arranged to take us to the only place in Thailand where I'd made reservations ahead of time, a private home called Bangrak House that would be our residence for the next few days. Once outside the airport doors, I was immediately hit with culture shock: the chaos and humidity and heat, the smells and racing motorbikes and buses and tuk-tuk drivers all but pulling you into their funky little taxis.

Everyone we spoke to who had traveled to Thailand warned us that Bangkok was loud, hot, and overwhelming and that we should get out as quickly as possible, but my culinary intuition told me that we needed to tough it out and stay for a few days. Bangkok is a melting pot of all things Southeast Asia and offers every type of Thai food imaginable from all regions of the country, and I wanted to take advantage of that. Also, our group was tough and able to deal with anything that came our way, so we decided to embrace the crazy. All nine of us can handle anything together—that's what teams do and what families do—and we are not afraid to jump in with both feet. Thailand may not have been our home or our country, but what we do not

understand shouldn't create fear but rather the desire to show respect and honor for the people who call this country home. We all wanted to be immersed in Thai culture, and this was step one.

The humidity and heat, however? There really is no way to get used to that; you just have to figure out how to survive it. As we waited for our ride for what seemed like an eternity, the kids were crumpled on the sidewalk, laying down on the dirt and grime, and none of us really even cared because the humidity does that to you. It sucks you dry and leaves you as limp as a rag doll. We were all glistening with sweat, tired, and bedraggled, and it was one funky crew that crawled into the van when it finally appeared.

Bangrak House 32

Our first destination was called Bangrak House 32, located in the Bangrak Districk of Bangkok, very close to the water taxis, the sky train, and shopping. The house itself was a hundred-year-old Chinese/Thai row house that had three narrow, steep flights of stairs and bedrooms with hard mattresses and windows that opened out into the Bangkok streets. I'd found this location on a popular vacation rental website, and I was excited to start our trip by staying in a traditional dwelling right in the heart of Bangkok. The owners of the home, Mac (a Westerner) and Noi, also owned a small bistro around the corner called Enjoy. The van dropped us off in front of Enjoy and we literally stumbled in, where our hosts greeted us with cocktails made with fresh fruit and steaming plates of our first Thai food. Spice and lime and sweet collided, and Rowan lay half asleep in my lap and obviously a little confused from the sights, smells, and heat. The kids all begged for more juice—which is a treat anyway—and more water, anything to save them from the humidity that felt as if it were pressing on our souls. Fortunately they were distracted from their misery by the cat that lived at Enjoy, which was running in and out and narrowly escaped getting hit by a racing scooter.

After we ate, our hosts led us down a narrow *soi* (small street) to the house, where we climbed up even narrower, steep stairs to find our rooms, which thankfully had much-needed air conditioning and ceiling fans. A dear friend had advised us not to use the air conditioning units during the day in order to acclimate to the humidity and heat, but in order to sleep at all, air conditioning was an absolute must.

Cooking with Nusi

We woke the next morning to the sounds of cheerful chatter from outside, and I looked out our bedroom window (no screens, just a plummeting three-story drop) and saw a woman cleaning squid in the street and a man scraping the scales off several fish. Baskets and buckets of vegetables sat nearby, and the smell of delicious food mixed with some not-so-pleasant smells filled my nostrils. The owner of a local cooking school had offered me his full attention for the day, starting with a market tour before cooking a long list of authentic Thai dishes, including making our own coconut cream, coconut milk, and curry paste. Mike, John, and I grabbed a cab and headed out to meet Nusi, our guide and teacher for the day, and the fun and excitement began.

I had no idea what to expect. I was in Southeast Asia for the first time, in the huge city of Bangkok, about to dive headfirst into my first Thai open-air market, and everywhere around me were sights, sounds, smells, and experiences that I wanted to soak in. There was no time to be jet-lagged and no easing into our surroundings. The market that Nusi took us to was next to a Hindu temple called Sri Mariamman Temple, and each detail of the temple was so ornate and interesting that I could have spent the entire day studying the architecture. But Nusi was walking fast, on a mission, and I learned quickly that he was in charge and was anxious to show me his skills and knowledge about Thai food.

Just a few minutes into this first market trip with Nusi, my love affair with Thailand began. Walking through the market was just a normal day for Nusi, but my senses were working overtime trying to take it all in. The market was

nothing like what most Westerners associate with the word *market*. There are few grocery stores to be found in Thailand, unless you consider a 7-Eleven to be a grocery store. Instead there are outdoor markets, some of which are open twenty-four hours a day, selling everything from fresh fruit, vegetables, and meat to live fish, frogs, and turtles (which are not to be eaten but purchased and released for good karma). You can also find prepared food at these markets: woks sizzling with stir-frys, meat on a stick, bags of sticky rice, crackling fried pork skins, poultry, confections made of rice or coconut milk, and fermented, pickled, and dried foods, some of which looked and smelled amazing and some whose smell alone could make you gag.

Nusi has owned his own cooking school, Silom Thai Cooking School, for more than ten years, and he now employs several instructors. I was truly honored that after I had contacted him to explain our mission, he decided to give us a private lesson showcasing his skills as a chef and teacher. Nusi is hilarious, animated, and quick to share his knowledge. During our tour through the market, Nusi would stop and pick up items like Thai basil and other fresh herbs whose strong scents made me almost dizzy. Suddenly there was lemongrass

and kaffir limes in my hands and Nusi was explaining that one must use specific ingredients to make real Thai food and substitutes are just that, substitutes, and I was already wondering how I was going to re-create these dishes back at home. Nusi filled our basket with bright chiles of varying size, fresh seafood, vegetables I had never seen before, several types of basil, sawtooth coriander, and the cutest little bananas I had ever seen. The most memorable part of our market trip was when Nusi cut into a kaffir lime that immediately squirted me directly in the eye. Not wanting to make Nusi feel bad, I tried to hide my reaction, but I was laughing and crying simultaneously as Nusi explained how strong the juice of the kaffir lime is and that it's not typically eaten but used for medicinal purposes or for cleaning. As he chattered, distracted and walking, I was experiencing firsthand the medicinal effects of kaffir lime as it burned like fire in my eye.

We left the market with our basket of goods and hurried to keep up with Nusi. I kept looking at everything around us all at once, trying to take it all in. Nusi hailed a taxi and we all crammed into the thankfully air-conditioned car and headed for Nusi's cooking school. Once there, Nusi lead us down a little *soi* (street) that was all small houses crammed together. Each house had a tiny garden out front that was spilling over with plants, flowers, and drying clothes, and some had birdcages with little birds inside, singing the sweetest songs I had ever heard. We found out later that these birds are raised to be singers and the owners enter them in competitions for prize money.

When we arrived at Nusi's school, we walked into the most beautifully decorated little home-turned-classroom that I have ever seen. There were mortars and pestles, beautiful dishes, paintings, spices, walls covered with decorations, and finally, a gorgeous, giant teakwood table filling the center of the room, laid out with cooking tools, cutting boards, and various bowls of herbs, spices, and different kinds of rice. We

took our goods into a tiny room in the back of the school and washed everything we'd just purchased at the market. My lesson was about to begin.

Watching Nusi cook was like watching an artist at work. He was so fast and efficient, and he'd obviously grown up cooking the food of his heritage. We whipped up a creamy, spicy, tangy soup; I made my first papaya salad and pounded out some curry paste in a giant granite mortar and pestle (much harder than it sounds); and I learned the important rules of what sets Thai food apart from other cuisines. Nusi taught me that in order for Thai food to be truly Thai food, there must be a balance of sweet, spicy, salty, savory, and sometimes bitter. Within that balance, though, Nusi explained that you should cook your food according to what you like.

My senses were working overtime as I tasted chiles hotter than any I had ever tasted before and

ate Thai food that was out-of-this-world delicious. Mike snapped pictures and John took furious notes, but nothing could truly capture our first day in Thailand. Nusi gave us such an amazing experience and willingly shared with us his passion for food and for his culture. I can't wait to return and see Nusi again and visit his amazing little school in the heart of the bustle and crazy that is Bangkok.

After our first day of cooking we were exhausted as the jetlag began to kick in. Heading back to our row house, I truly felt like I was in a dream. Having left my comfort zone and landed in a place completely different from what I was used to, I found it very hard to place myself in the moment and sometimes got a sense of floating along through time. (I'm sure being tired beyond all reason doesn't help with that sensation either.) The kids, America, and Mayela were all happy, hot, sweaty, and glad to see us back. They had had adventures of their own: hunting down food from street vendors, having their first Thai smoothie made with exotic fruits, and seeing, smelling, and hearing things they never had been exposed to before. We all sprawled across the two beds in the room that John, the boys, and I were staying in and talked about our day. I was so grateful to be on this trip with these amazing people, and I could tell already that we would be seeing the world differently when we left and that experiencing this trip with my family and friends that I love so dearly would truly be a dream come true.

This night was the first of many with all of us crammed together, laughing, sharing, and just being.

Cooking with Ninja

Our next cooking adventure was with the chef at the bistro, Enjoy, owned by our gracious hosts, Mac and Noi. They were thrilled when I asked if I could learn a few recipes from Ninja, who was Noi's cousin, and after watching his knife skills, I can vouch that he was aptly named.

Ninja was in his twenties and had grown up in southern Thailand. He lost both of his parents at a very young age and was raised by family members, and he learned his craft by helping them out in the kitchen. Ninja's cooking style was a mixture of southern and northern, his flavors were consistent, and like a true chef, he tested and tasted every dish before serving anything to his customers. I cooked for three straight days with Ninja outside in the open-air bistro, and as I wilted in the heat, trying to keep track of Ninja's amazing skills and fast preparation, I realized that although he was several years younger than I, I was learning from a true master.

Ninja knew no English and was shy and quiet, but as we continued to cook together, he would look up and smile, and when I showed my appreciation for his delicious food, he would beam with pride and move on confidently to his next amazing creation. Working with Ninja, Noi, and the rest of the staff at Enjoy, we began to learn and understand more and more about Thai culture. Although they are extremely nice, welcoming, and attentive, Thai people are not as quick to be affectionate as Americans generally are. This does not mean that they are uncaring or lack warmth; it just reflects a Thai sense of formality. Everyone we met did, however, display genuine affection for our children. They were all fussed over and talked to, cheeks softly caressed and words of admiration showered upon them. Children are cherished in Thailand, and our experience with the people we encountered and our children were all extremely positive.

The most important lesson I took away from my time cooking with Ninja is to taste as you go when creating the flavors that are Thai food. Unfortunately, monosodium glutamate (MSG) is widely used in Thai cooking, but thankfully Ninja relied on his family's instructions to taste as you go and season accordingly. Like Nusi, Ninja balanced the flavors in Thai food by tasting and then adjusting the seasoning, and I found this reassuring for my own style of cooking back home. Recipes should be a foundation for how you want your food to taste, not the be-all and end-all of what to put in each dish.

I must pause here and give a giant thank you to all of our Bangkok friends: Nusi and everyone as Silom Cooking School, Noi, Mac, Ninja, and all the friendly and welcoming staff at Enjoy Bistro. Each of you went above and beyond to help us with our quest, and in just the few short days of our visit I learned more than I could have imagined about your amazing culture, food, and the city of Bangkok. I will never forget our experiences together, and I am forever grateful.

The Chatuchak Weekend Market

Besides cooking in Bangkok, we also took time to visit the zoo and toured an amazing market the size of eight football fields (over 35 acres) called the Chatuchak Weekend Market. The market was the most overwhelming place I have ever been to, and I felt immediately that if we did not have Ninja and Noi as our guides, there was a good chance that we would wander into the market and never be seen again. Around every corner was something we had never seen before. The children tried their first rambutan and dragon fruit, and we watched live fish flopping with vigor, splashing the kids with salty water and making them squeal and jump. We witnessed live frogs being whacked on the head, gutted, and skinned in three seconds flat; stray dogs stealing fresh meat; and men pushing giant, and I mean *giant*, baskets brimming with green leafy vegetables through narrow stalls, nearly running us over as

we were eager to see everything but what was about to kill us. People maneuvered through the narrow market streets on scooters, brushing against us and reminding us that this was not home. My farmers market does not allow dogs or bicycles, much less motorized scooters! The kids hung in there for two hours in the melting humidity; the air-conditioned taxis we took back to the Bangrak house saved us. As I type this, I am swept back to the madness, charm, and beauty of the market trip with Noi and Ninja.

Thai Massage

Also while in Bangkok, we experienced our first massages! After a long day with the kids at the zoo and exploring our neighborhood by foot, we walked by a massage studio that had several professionally dressed women waiting by comfortable reclining chairs as cool air rushed out of the tidy, cutely decorated room. We tumbled in, embarrassed about our dirty feet but excited for some pampering. The ladies were delighted that we had the kids with us and hurried to prepare us for our foot massages. They first washed our feet with warm water, and as I stared down at my swollen toes I realized how much the humidity was taking its toll on our bodies, along with the jet lag and most likely dehydration. In that humidity, it was simply impossible to stay hydrated. Our kids were all smiles at the awesomeness of a foot massage, and we were right there with them. I was overwhelmed with pleasure and happiness, and glad that we could all be together after the first few days of our Thailand adventure. Rowan and Cat fell asleep during their massages, which meant a long walk back carrying the two sleepyheads, but it was well worth it. Those foot massages began our appreciation for the art of Thai massage, and we very much took advantage of having such a luxury available at an affordable price. While in Thailand, you must experience Thai massage for yourself—not only does it feel great, you'll also help support the hardworking men and women in this honorable profession.

Chiang Mai

After four days in Bangkok, we had started to acclimate (a little) to the humidity, smells, and culture, and although we were enjoying our stay in the crazy huge city, we knew that we would be returning to Bangkok for our flight home, so together we decided it was time to head north. Our friends who spend a lot of time in Thailand said Chiang Mai could not be passed up: amazing food, friendly people, awesome beauty, and cooler weather. Because we had no set plans, it took us a day to find flights and to reserve a place to stay. I did a little Internet research and found Awanahouse, a cool little hotel situated right in the heart of Chiang Mai, within the walls of the "old city" and only a block away from the famous Sunday night Walking Street market. We were all very excited for the next leg of our journey!

Awanahouse

When we arrived in Chiang Mai, it was astounding how different it felt from Bangkok. The air was cleaner, we flew into a jungle-like setting, and it was much less crowded, even in the busy airport. Mike and John finagled a van to take us to our hotel, and we were off! Awanahouse was cute, clean, and incredibly inexpensive. The location was even better than we had hoped, the food was amazing, and the pool was shaded from the tropical sun so our kids could swim for hours without turning into little lobsters.

The only downside? We. Were. Loud. Our group of nine swallowed the tiny place up. We were also respectful and kind, but a guest at Awanahouse saw us arrive with four kids in tow and immediately complained that she feared we would keep her awake. Silly fear, trust me, the kids being jet-lagged little bugs who were often asleep by 7 p.m. and sometimes earlier, although they were up at the crack of dawn. We stayed at Awanahouse for a night and enjoyed their services, but with yet another warning that the same guest was "worried that we may become annoying," we decided to find a place to stay that was a bit more welcoming to our brood. But if you're traveling to Chiang Mai (without nine people or four children), I fell in love with Awanahouse and highly recommend it. It's most definitely a couple's retreat or a backpacker's oasis, but you simply can't beat the price of the lodging and food, and I'm confident we will visit Awanahouse again.

Baanpong Lodge

Eager to find a new and larger location, America, Mike, John, and I left the children in Mayela's care while we went to search for a new place to call home. We were hoping for our own house within the city but kept coming up empty-handed. Our ride for the day was a nice gentleman who drove a songtao (a pickup truck with cushioned seats in the truck bed). The songtaos were the best way to get around in Chiang Mai, and we found a driver who was willing, for a reasonable set rate, to stick with us for the day as we searched for better lodging. We ended up about fifteen miles out of town, where there was a beautiful and affordable villa for rent. It was too secluded, though, and I needed to find someone to cook with and learn from!

We left feeling a bit unsure about what to do. In the end, we asked for a recommendation from the owner of a roadside stand who really didn't understand us at all, but somehow Mike, John, the songtao driver, and the roadside stand owner all managed to communicate that we needed lodging that was kid-friendly, preferably with a pool. The roadside stand owner explained something to the songtao driver, and we were once again on our way. We had no idea where we were headed, but the songtao driver seemed confident, and that exchange ended up leading us to a sanctuary that turned out to be our home for the next ten days: Baanpong Lodge.

As we pulled into the secluded parking lot of Baanpong Lodge, it was as if we had arrived at the gates of heaven. We walked up a narrow path, turned the corner, and were faced with a beautiful pool, two rows of what looked like little townhomes, a lovely outside dining area with a bar, and a cute little outdoor kitchen. The owner, Nim, a beautiful and sweet young woman, greeted us warmly. Their only guests had left and the place was quiet and vacant except for the staff. It was the off-season, so although they had visitors come up for the food, drinks, and a plunge in the pool, overnight guests were minimal. Perfect for us, and a wonderful negotiating tool! After looking at the beautiful rooms, we decided to sample their menu. The food was fresh, alive with flavor, and downright delicious. It was like a dream come true: great food, vacant rooms, sparkling pool, gorgeous backdrop, and a welcoming spirit on the part of the staff. It all combined to make us feel like we were home.

We asked Nim if she would let us stay for several days, cook with their chef to learn some of her amazing recipes, and take photographs of the food as we learned. Nim introduced us at that point to her husband, Henrick, a quiet and kind man from South Africa, and they both agreed that they would love to have us. The entire place was ours! We couldn't wait to retrieve the kids and Mayela and introduce them to our little slice of paradise. Just typing this makes me miss our Chiang Mai retreat, the friendly staff, the comfortable rooms, the awesome food, and the warm pool. We stayed at Baanpong for several days, cooking with

Chef Jim (a lovely woman), enjoying the pool, and falling in love with Chiang Mai's beauty.

Chef Jim is an accomplished chef who started her career after culinary school as a hotel chef for one of the larger five-star corporations in Thailand, where she worked for ten years before Nim and Heinrick recruited her. She was excited to have a job closer to home and with a more flexible schedule so that she could spend more time with her family. Now that she has taken her culinary training to the small resort that is Baanpong, even during the off-season travelers and locals alike make the trek from Chiang Mai and nearby villages for the delicious food that comes from Chef Jim's kitchen, not

to mention the peace and serenity of this awesome little resort. Finding this place was truly a gift. I learned so much from Chef Jim. Although she knew very little English, Nim was happy to translate for her, and we spent several hours together in the small outdoor kitchen as I watched her create amazing dishes, several of which are in this book. Like the other chefs I worked with in Thailand, Jim always put the emphasis on fresh ingredients, and on her weekly trips to the market she always brought back the best veggies, meat, and seafood she could find. Fresh and locally sourced ingredients are the secret to amazing food, and the reality is, there is no secret—it's all about living as sustainably as possible and as close to your food source as you can get. Baanpong also had its own small garden that Chef Jim used for some ingredients, which was simply awesome.

Mark Ritchie and ISDSI

We were so lucky while staying at Baanpong to have Henrick offer us the use of his van, because we were rather far from the actual city of Chiang Mai. After being at Baanpong for a few days, we were all getting a bit antsy for the bustle of our cool neighboring city, and I really wanted a chance to lift some weights. A quick Google search brought up CrossFit Chiang Mai, and I almost slapped myself on the forehead because seeing the owner's name, Mark Ritchie, jolted the memory that I had corresponded with him a year or so earlier. Mark, who is from America, had contacted me to discuss the possibility of my coming to Chiang Mai for a Paleo event. At that point in my life the idea was impossible, and now here I was in his town and I hadn't even reached out before we left! I felt like a huge jerk as I timidly sent Mark a Facebook message, and almost immediately I received a response. The next day we scooped up the kiddos and headed in his direction, excited to meet someone from home and to be in a familiar environment. In the end, what we got from Mark was so much more than a great workout—he gave us a gift that could not be matched.

Mark Ritchie greeted us at the door to his gym and warmly welcomed us inside. (Actually, the heat and humidity already had us feeling pretty warm, but we appreciated his friendliness and generosity.) Mark's gym was wonderful and professional, and employed excellent coaches. How cool to find a place like this right in the heart of Chiang Mai! Mark's true passion, however, was his day job, running the International Sustainable Development Studies Institute (ISDSI).

Mark founded ISDSI for students who want to study abroad and are interested in anthropology, environmental studies, biology, and other disciplines. The program is remarkable and emphasizes that the students show respect and honor to the Thai people that they work with. As Mark explained to me, the focus of the program and its courses is sustainability. Students live in small Thai villages and the villagers teach the students about their culture and practices, with an emphasis on sustainable agriculture and food systems. For the students, this becomes an arsenal of information that can help us in the West marry our culture and sound ecological practices in order to live more sustainably. The villagers who are involved in this program are valued. They understand the important role they have in helping us change the way we live for the better. Sometimes the "old way" of doing things is the best way, and unfortunately the way we live in the West today is not always good for our environment or our future.

Often visitors come to remote villages from other programs and instead of listening and learning, they want to change the "old ways." ISDSI students have no agenda except to learn from the practices of the villages that are living sustainably. Many of the villages involved with the ISDSI program are helping to keep our earth green. They stay in one place for only a short period of time, moving the village through the forest so that the forest can regrow where they lived, and maintaining a sustainable lifestyle. I was so excited to get to know Mark better; immediately after meeting him I already wished that we had more time to spend with him and his wonderful family.

After our workout we stayed for CrossFit Chiang Mai's weekly Saturday barbecue, which consisted of an awesome Paleo meal of grilled meats, veggies, salads, and insects. Yes, insects. Edible crawlers are a widely accepted form of protein and have been used as a nutrient-dense protein source in rural Thai communities for centuries. Today, not as many Thai people rely on insects for protein, but it's still fairly common

to find several varieties of the fried and spiced critters in markets, homes, and, well, potlucks! Jaden and Mike were over the moon to try the crickets and worms, and John and I were willing if less-excited participants. What can I say, insects are not steak, but they are also, I admit, not bad. Thai spices are very forgiving of whatever they are flavoring, so that at least was on my side. I do believe that insect consumption could truly help end world hunger, and I'm all for it—it's a resource that needs to be explored. In the meantime, I'm okay with not making insects my main source of protein, but learning more about the cultural relevance of eating insects in Asia and trying them myself was a truly epic part of our experience. This would not be our only encounter with edible insects, but it was definitely memorable.

During the potluck, Mark made us an incredible offer to have two of his ISDSI employees, Am and Gene, take us to an organic, fully self-sustaining farm in the small village of Mae Ta for a visit and lunch the next day. He also offered to take us to his favorite market in Chiang Mai the day after our farm trip. Of course we jumped on the opportunity, and we left CrossFit Chiang Mai happy to have made the connection with Mark and his family and excited about our adventures that lay ahead.

The Farm in Mae Ta

Early the next morning, we made our way down to the parking lot of our cozy hideaway and clambered into the van with Am and Gene. We started the long journey north to Mae Ta, where we would spend the day on the sustainable farm. Am explained to us that our visit would be less a tour than an introduction to the daily life of the family who ran the farm. I felt completely honored to be given this opportunity, and I was filled with an overwhelming sense of joy at the kindness displayed by these wonderful people who were wiling to let complete strangers intrude on their world.

We drove deeper into the jungle until we finally arrived at our destination. The location was beyond beautiful. The farmhouse was a gorgeous teak wood construction that sat high on stilts, and underneath was a large patio with tables, chairs, and tools.

As we unloaded from the van, Am introduced us to a lovely older woman named Paw Paat and her adult daughter, Mae Saun, who helped run the farm. Paw Paat's husband was away, traveling around the country to help other small farmers learn how to create more sustainable and organic practices.

The history of the farm that we were visiting was extremely interesting and inspiring. Years before, the government had mandated that the farm grow tobacco and the family complied, to the extreme detriment of the family's and laborers' health. The harsh chemicals and pesticides that were used were making everyone sick, and they longed for the days of organic farming and living off of their own land. They decided to go back to the traditional ways of farming, and although the government did not support their choice, they insisted. It's been a long and difficult journey, but today they are farming their land the way they want to and are thriving and healthy again because of that choice. Their mission now is to help others who feel the same way and to provide information and assistance to the families who want to protect their sustainable and organic farming practices rather than grow subsidized crops through practices that harm the well being of the farmers and laborers.

I was so inspired to hear this story that it brought tears to my eyes. As I watched Mae Saun and Paw Paat lead my little boys out to the fields, heads held high with pride, I knew this was a day I would never forget.

We had not strayed far from the house when we stopped next to several pineapple plants. Paw Paat used a large machete to cut off two pineapples that still looked a bit green, but she seemed confident that they were ready. Growing a pineapple is no easy feat. Am explained to us that in order to grow a pineapple you first need, well, a pineapple; you cut off the top and plant it. All well and good, but it can take up to three years before it starts to bear fruit, and a single pineapple plant only produces one fruit a year, so it takes a lot of patience and a lot of plants to get multiple pineapples per year. Learning this made us all feel very honored that they were willing to share two of their pineapples with us, because quite honestly, they did not have a vast number of plants that I could see.

We took the pineapples back to the porch under the house and Mae Saun immediately started cutting the fruit into slices. Our children's little eager hands were soon filled with the juicy goodness of what I thought looked like a not-yet-ripe pineapple. Rowan's huge eyes after his first bite told me otherwise. When I could get through our clambering, pineapple-deranged children to try a slice myself, I simply could not believe what I tasted. I can't even describe the flavor or experience with words. It was simply out-of-this-world amazing. I will never eat another bite of pineapple again without comparing it to the sweet, luscious, silky deliciousness that was the pineapple we ate on the farm that day.

After our fruit feast, we ventured back out onto the farm and this time headed for large shoots of what looked like bamboo. It turned out to be a different type of shoot, and although we tried to get its name, no one was really able to translate or even tell us exactly what it was! Paw Paat took her machete and cut off a large piece of a shoot. She deftly chopped away at the hard, dark outside of the shoot until she exposed a creamy

They were tender, mild, and delightful, and it was so much fun to eat flowers in the beautiful fields. After our baskets were full we walked back to the house on a leafy path, and Mae Saun began to harvest the large leaves that bordered the back of the porch. They looked almost like huge spinach leaves but were a darker green and teardrop-shaped, and we were told they were pak miang leaves and would be part of our meal. We now had everything we needed to make lunch!

We huddled around Paw Paat as she sat on her low stool, almost in a squat, and watched her prepare the shoot. I tried to cut it along with her, but my unskilled hands next to hers were almost comical. She held a small piece of the shoot flat in her palm and sliced away with a small knife. My first try left me with a small cut, which I tried to hide thanks to my utter embarrassment, so I reverted to my own American way of using a little cutting board that she gave to me after witnessing my blunder. After the shoots were cut, Paw Paat let them soak in water and turned to the curry paste prep. In her mortar and pestle she combined fresh chiles, turmeric, and shrimp paste, and then a small chicken (already dead and plucked) appeared and she began to break it down. She cut up everything between the beak and the feet, including the edible innards such as the liver, kidneys, and heart, and everything that could be chewed and swallowed went into a pot.

softer center, and she gestured to us that this is what we would eat! We took the shoot back to the porch for later and ventured back out to the fields, where we found rows of beautiful, small purple flowers. We were handed baskets and instructed to harvest the little purple jewels. Am told us that they were called butterfly pea flowers and could be eaten raw or cooked, or made into tea or a cool, refreshing drink, Once the kids heard we could eat them, they all started munching away on the flowers, and of course we had to try them as well.

Over the chicken went water and the curry paste, and she set it to boil on a small two-burner propane stove. As the curry worked its magic on the chicken, Paw Paat started preparing the flowers. In a large wok she stir-fried the flowers with oyster sauce, added several eggs, and expertly created a stunning scramble that glowed deep purple from the flowers. Mae Saun soaked another basket of flowers in hot water to make a tea. It turned out to taste more like lemonade, and the kids simply could not get enough of the lavender goodness in a glass. Finally, the chopped-up shoots were added to the chicken curry and the pak miang leaves were prepared in a scramble just like the flowers. It was time to feast, and feast we did, outside on the porch under the beautiful teak house, looking out over the farm that was tended with heart and soul by this amazing family who had, against all odds, fulfilled their dream to live simply from the land and to take care of their family members by doing what they knew was best for their bodies and for the earth that provided them with all that they needed. I will never forget our day at the farm, and thank you again to Mark Ritchie for providing us with the opportunity.

Warorot Market

Speaking of Mark, I was honored that the day after our trip to the farm, Mark agreed to spend a day with us, taking us to his favorite market and telling us about Thai culture and the experiences that led him to live in Thailand. The introduction to this book was greatly enhanced by our time spent with Mark and his understanding of Thai culture. Furthermore, our day wandering the Warorot Market with Mark was by far one of the best days we had in Thailand. It was so great to have his perspective and knowledge, and it was with Mark that we were able to sample some of the best street food that we had on our trip, including the pork rinds that you will find a recipe for on page 90. If you ever travel to Chiang Mai, this is the market you must visit. It's where the Thai people shop themselves, and it gives you a glimpse of how life is lived in this amazing country. Our visit there was a truly unbelievable experience of the sights, sounds, smells, and crazy beauty and intensity that is Thailand.

Cooking with Pom

Our last cooking experience in Chiang Mai was with the beautiful Pom, owner and founder of Cooking@home Thai Culinary School. I found Pom via her website and knew I would love her even before we met. Pom teaches cooking classes at her home in Sankhampaeng, a small village outside of Chiang Mai. Her setup was absolutely beautiful: the kitchen was outside, of course, on a lovely covered porch with plenty of room to move around and an unbelievable view of the fields surrounding her home and the green hills that are the backdrop of Chiang Mai. Pom explained to us that Thai people learn to cook from their family members and cooking is a skill passed on from generation to generation. She learned to cook herself by being constantly at her mother's side, and her love for food led her to her first job in the culinary world in 1993 as an instructor at the Chiang Mai Thai Cookery School.

In 2009, Pom decided to branch out on her own, and with the help of her husband, she now runs her very successful cooking school from her own kitchen. Pom shares with her students her favorite family recipes, and cooking with her was truly one of the highlights of our trip. She encourages her students to taste as they cook, not just to make sure that what they are creating tastes good, although that's important, but also to let them enjoy the process. My favorite dish that I learned from Pom has to be the pumpkin custard found on page 212. It's fun, creative, delicious, and super nutritious for a treat. I'm excited to share with you everything that I learned from Pom in the recipe section of this book.

A Muay Thai Fight

We ended up staying in Chiang Mai for almost ten days total. It honestly began to feel like home. We fell in love with the city, the kindness of the people, the Walking Street market, the food, the beauty, the amazing massages, and the culture. One of the most memorable experiences of our time in Chiang Mai, besides what I've already shared with you, was the Muay Thai fight we attended in the heart of downtown at the local Muay Thai arena.

John and Mike reserved tables for us close to the ring so that we could be right next to the action. My boys are both karate students and we have a long history of being involved with marital arts on some level, but even so, we were all completely moved by what we witnessed that evening.

The history of Muay Thai is long and complicated. There are conflicting ideas about the origins of Muay Thai, but most agree that it was used several hundred years ago by Thai warriors during combat. Today, Muay Thai is practiced by fighters around the world and is honored as one of the most effective forms of self-defense. It combines punching and kicking, and fighters can use their fists, knees, elbows, and feet.

Muay Thai is deeply rooted in Thai tradition and culture, and before each fight the fighters wear a ceremonial headdress and perform a dance called *ram muay* to show respect to the opposing fighter, opposing camp, and their own instructors, parents, teachers, and sometimes religious beliefs. The dance can also showcase the fighter's skills. Traditional music called *sarama* is played during

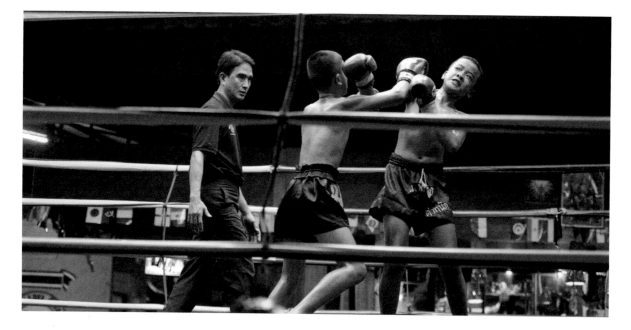

the pre-fight ceremony and during the fights to keep the fighters motivated and the crowd excited. The beating of the drums and the chanting voices are riveting and create a sense of excitement that is contagious.

As we entered the fighting stadium, it was dark, hot, and already getting crowded. The kids were soaking it all in, and as the first fight started I realized that the fighters couldn't be much older than Jaden—they looked like they were maybe only ten or eleven. I have since learned that boys typically start to train in Muay Thai at the age of four and often start fighting in the ring by ten. Sometimes Muay Thai fighters will have up to 200 fights under their belt by the time they reach their twenties. That's more fights than most professional boxers compete in during their entire lifetime! The heart, the drive, the discipline that was portrayed by the two young fighters was extremely moving. I experienced a strange flood of emotions watching the two young men battle. I couldn't imagine watching my own boys fight in the ring with no pads or protective gear at such a young age, but I also knew this event was taking place within a completely different kind of upbringing and philosophy. These kids were deeply embedded in over five hundred years of

Muay Thai history. I am not one to pass judgment on something like this, which is so ingrained, honored, and expected within Thai culture. These boys were simply competing at their sport and doing it well, with pride and confidence. It was rather amazing to watch, and I found myself overwhelmed with emotion. Watching my boys take it all in was also emotional; little Rowan and Jaden were both wide-eyed, tucked under John's arms, tired but wide awake from the action, my little warriors safe with us in our seats, never having to battle besides in play. They were witnessing a display full of cultural meaning, and although I knew it was a lot for them to process, it was an incredible experience for us all.

The rest of the night was pure excitement as the fighters who came next were older and more experienced. Our kids were able to meet several of them afterward, and they were all gracious and kind and willing to let us all take pictures with them. The hard work and dedication displayed by each fighter and the obvious honor and respect that they all had for each other was a great lesson for all of us. No matter what we choose to do with our lives, we must give it our all and do it well, and whether we win or lose, we should be proud of who we are and what we have accomplished.

Khao Lak

After Chiang Mai, we decided to head south so that we could experience southern Thai cuisine and the beauty of Thailand's coast and islands. We really had no idea where we wanted to go, but since we were there during the off-season, we knew that weather could be an issue, especially in Phuket. Mark Ritchie had suggested that we stay north of Phuket in a city called Khao Lak. Our plan was to fly into Phuket and stay there for a few days, but with Mark's tip, we decided to take the same flight and drive up to Khao Lak. The small town is popular with divers and other vacationers who want to get away from the craziness of Phuket, and it's only an hour's drive north of Phuket on the west coast of mainland Thailand, in the province of Phang Nga.

One of Mark's employees had a family member who knew the chef at a resort called Ayara Villas, which was situated directly on the beach and booming with people during peak season, but when we arrived, it was completely dead. Upon our arrival, we were excited to see that walking out the back patio of the rooms led you directly into the pool. No joke, the water was the back porch, and although it was only few inches deep right out of the door, another six feet took you right into the deep end. The kids were immediately in the water and pretty much stayed there for the entire two days that we were in Khao Lak. Traveling during the off-season definitely has its perks (even though the beaches were rough and dangerous and the weather was muggy, sticky, and *hot*), and the price of our beautiful accommodations was truly unbelievable.

The very kind chef at Ayara Villas agreed to meet with us so that I could learn any recipes she might have to share. I had gathered several recipes already and specifically wanted to learn southern-style dishes. But after meeting with her and seeing what dishes she could teach me, we decided that it would be better to not spend our limited time in Khao Lak cooking with her. Although I'm sure we would have had a wonderful time, the items that she had on her menu to show us were all dishes that I had already learned. The only thing to do at this point was to explore the little town we were staying in to see if there were any cooking schools or restaurants specializing in southern Thai cuisine that might be willing to work with us. Mike, America, John, and I left the kids with Mayela to swim in the beautiful pool and took off for town on foot. About a mile down the road, we were wilting from the humidity, so we made it our mission to find motor scooters for rent. Our search eventually bore fruit, and I jumped on the back of one scooter with John while America joined Mike and we were off. I felt like a little girl pretending to not be afraid as I held on to John and prayed that he knew what he was doing. We had no idea where we were headed, but at least we were no longer walking. Thus began our affection for motor scooters. It was also a moment of epiphany: we finally understood why practically everyone in Thailand rides one! First, scooters provide you with nature's air conditioner, turning hot and humid Thailand into a tropical paradise as you whiz down the road, cooled by the speed. Second, obviously, you can get where you need to go a heck of a lot faster than walking. Third, you can squeeze into tight places and down little alleys, and you suddenly feel like you belong in Thailand, speeding around dangerously on two tiny wheels, ignoring all traffic laws and feeling a little bit bad and imagining that you are invincible.

We drove up and down quite a few streets until we found a little, almost American-looking coffee shop. We stopped in and ordered iced coffees from the cute and sweet waitress, who was obviously wondering what the heck we were doing there during the off-season. She spoke surprisingly great English and introduced herself to us as Poo. We explained to Poo our mission and asked her if she knew of anyone in the area who might be able to teach us some southern Thai dishes. Without hesitation she told us about her good friends A and Bow, who had recently opened a little roadside restaurant called A.O Seafood that catered to the locals. Poo made a call, and before we knew it we were back on our scooters, heading down the street to meet A and Bow. Our next adventure had begun!

Cooking with A and Bow

A and Bow knew we were coming of course, because of the phone call from Poo, but our communication was silly at best because we knew very little Thai and only A knew a tiny bit of English. However, they understood our purpose, and the first thing to do was obvious: they wanted to make sure we liked their food!

As we sat at the humble plastic table waiting to see what Bow would bring us, we took in our surroundings. The restaurant was really just a tin roof over a cement slab, which was attached to the motor scooter repair shop next door. A small wall in the back of the restaurant separated the kitchen from the dining area, and our view was of scooters and cars whizzing by the busy road out front. It was a classic Thailand restaurant experience.

Bow emerged quickly from the back with a plate piled with small shrimp swimming in a curry sauce, with what look like giant lima beans on the side. It turned out that they were stink beans, a staple ingredient in southern Thai cooking. The dish was amazing. Spicy and savory flavors mingled and swam together, kaffir lime hit our noses as chiles started to burn, and then there was the sweet coolness from the shrimp. Yes. We would learn a lot from this little gem tucked away in the quiet of off-season Khao Lak. We arranged to come back the next day, and A and Bow offered to close their restaurant just for us in order to teach us as many dishes as possible. I was astounded and excited. What a stroke of luck! Poo had called Bow again while we were there to make

sure we had found them, and she offered to come the next day with her friend Joe to help translate. I couldn't believe their kindness. Everyone was so eager to help and accommodate us, complete strangers with a strange agenda. We headed back to Ayara Villas excited for tomorrow's lesson in southern Thai cuisine!

The next day was a little like a dream. I felt like we were seriously embedded at this point into Thai culture, and these young people's excitement and passion about stories, food, and culture was almost palpable. Bow cooked several dishes for us; some, I will admit, were a bit too exotic for my taste, but unless you grow up eating some of what they offered, it would take a very acquired taste to enjoy some of the more outlandish dishes we sampled, and I appreciated every single thing that they made for us. We learned about fermented fish gut sauce, and Bow sent a bottle home with me that I will never use in my cooking but will cherish forever. It was the kindest gesture, and although fish gut sauce sounds more like a prank, it's truly a beloved ingredient used in southern Thai cooking, and I was honored that they wanted to give me a bottle of their favorite sauce. We ate

strange local plants and ferns that were stirred into soups, and tasted curries that I had never seen or heard of before. I found a new love for shrimp paste, despite the strong smell, and for pak miang leaves and stink beans—yes, I really do like them! We ate a paste made of little dried, fermented fish pounded together with green chiles to make a fiery-hot dip for vegetables, and we slurped up a coconut milk soup that tasted like the Thai version of clam chowder (you'll find this amazing recipe on page 164).

Most importantly, Joe and Poo told us their story of the 2004 tsunami, which devastated Khao Lak—a story of survival and hope, rebuilding and family, friendship and hardship, and always looking towards the future and not back on what was lost. Staying true to Thai culture, they displayed no sadness, only smiles and gratitude for being alive. To the Thai people, life is a gift, not a right, and to be able to smile and be happy is what they strive for, no matter what the circumstances.

Even when recalling the horrifying event that killed thousands upon thousands of their people, friends, and family, they smiled and said, as we sat crying and listening, "No, no, it's okay, we moved on, we have rebuilt, it's okay, we are happy." What a huge lesson we learned that day about life and perspective: We are so lucky to be able to experience what we do each day, with good health, good friends, and the ones that we love. We never know what life might bring, but we should face it together and look forward to tomorrow, always remembering to smile and be happy.

Thank you so much, A, Bow, Poo, and Joe. We will never forget any of you, and we will always be grateful for the day you spent with us. We learned so much from all of you, and your amazing spirit, joy, and smiles will warm my heart for years to come. Readers, if you visit the beautiful shores of Khao Lak, please go visit A.O Seafood restaurant and tell A and Bow hello from all of us. You will not regret it.

The Gulf of Thailand

After our two days in Khao Lak, we were not sure what to do next. Going back to Phuket was an option, but we wanted to enjoy the ocean and the weather reports for Phuket were not looking good. We wanted to be able to swim safely with the kids, so we started asking around about where to go next.

We found another small coffee shop, and the Australian owner was more than happy to help us. He suggested we go to the Gulf of Thailand and check out the small islands there. He even called a friend on the island of Koh Phangan, who confirmed that the waters were calm and snorkeling was possible this time of year. We went for it. Why not? Our options and time in Thailand was starting to dwindle, so we might as well be island castaways for our last few days in paradise.

We took a flight to Koh Samui, the largest of the islands off the east coast of the Kra Isthmus. We were plopped in the middle of the Gulf of Thailand, and I was quite sure I would be content to be plopped there forever. We walked off the airplane onto what felt like a giant plush golf course, which I learned later is coincidentally how many people describe the island of Koh Samui. We knew we wanted to spend a few days on this, the largest island in the gulf, but first we wanted to explore Koh Phangan, the smaller island that's home to the Full Moon Party, a monthly celebration on the beach that draws 10,000 to 30,000 people. After landing, we took a shuttle to the ferry terminal and from there took a ferry over to Koh Phangan.

Koh Phangan

Koh Phangan had a very laid-back, small-village vibe, and as we stood on the dock looking around, we wondered what the heck we were supposed to do and where on earth we should go. There was not the usual taxi, tuk-tuk, and songtao parade waiting for the next rider to come along, but a woman walked up to us who was obviously paid to try and convince lost and sweaty tourists like ourselves into visiting the nearest resort swimming pool.

After some talking and haggling with the woman, who turned out to be quite nice and helpful, she told us about her "cousin's" place, Sandy Bay Bungalows, right on the beach and close to town. She said it was the only place that was very nice and also inexpensive and was located on the best beach. Of course we didn't know if what she said was true, but since we didn't know anything at all about Koh Phangan except what I had read online about the best parts of the island for snorkeling, we decided to check it out.

She somehow conjured up a songtao for us (I'm sure she had him waiting around the corner for her next tourist find) and told him where to take us. We arrived about forty-five minutes later at Sandy Bay Bungalows, and we were off on one of the final legs of our journey through Thailand.

Sandy Bay is one of the many reasons why I love Thailand. Our little retreat was plopped under a sloping green jungle hill that slides into soft white sand and ends in clear, blue-green water. Tucked onto the beach and up into the hills were tiny beach bungalows equipped with all you really needed to experience Thailand like you should: a bed, a small refrigerator, a bathroom, a window, and a porch—all for about $30 a night. Done. Where in the world can you get beachfront lodging in one of the most beautiful places anyone has ever seen for that price? Well, in Thailand, if you look hard enough, there is an inexpensive paradise around every corner.

The Sandy Bay office was connected to the kitchen, and the restaurant was, of course, open-air, though covered to shade you from the relentless tropical sun. Next to the restaurant was an awesome pool overlooking the beach and the sea. The resort was very quiet because it was the off-season and because this time of year, there were not any waves. But that was okay; the kids could splash happily on the beach and alternate between running after crabs and jumping in the pool. Nobody was complaining.

The owners of Sandy Bay found us hilarious. I'm still not sure if they were laughing at us or with us, but either way, they knew their location was amazing and that we would stay and laugh with them. The food we ate from their kitchen was scrumptious and affordable, and I had hopes that the staff would warm up to us enough that I could learn a few things from the chef.

Fortunately, our wishes came to fruition, and after a couple of days of eating their food and letting them help us arrange a few activities, we brought up the idea of cooking with the chef for an afternoon. They were a little confused until I showed them my last book, which helped them understand our mission, and they kindly obliged. We learned several dishes in this book from the chef at Sandy Bay Bungalows, and when you travel to Koh Phangan, I promise you will not find a better location or price. You must go and stay in the little bungalows by the sea and laugh with the owners as you relax and soak in the essence of Thailand.

We had a wild adventure while staying on Koh Phangan in the form of a boat trip to a well-known snorkeling location a few miles from shore. We thought we had rented a private boat, but it turned out we were sharing it with a few scuba divers. The boat was huge and had a top deck that was shaded on one half and a bottom deck that was constantly splashed and sprayed by the sea. The day we went out was rough, and although I never have been seasick before, by the time we reached our destination we all were about ten different shades of green.

Jaden and John bravely jumped in first, and I was scared out of my mind watching them bounce in the waves. They figured out a way for John to hold on to a life vest and for Jaden to hold on to John so they could snorkel without it taking too much effort to stay afloat in the not-so-calm seas. I could hardly watch. Rowan took one look and decided that he had no desire to try, and I was grateful that for once my brave boy opted out of an adventure. Mayela soon joined Jaden and John, and I was impressed and scared by their daring. America and the girls also opted out at first, but eventually Giana and Mike decided to make the jump into the sea. Now that they were in, I had no excuses. Mayela returned to the boat to watch Rowan and it was my turn. After watching nine-year-old Jaden bravely go for it, I had to at least try. It was scary, yes, but the decision to take the plunge into the unknown was totally worth it. The water was deep enough that you couldn't really make out the bottom, but the sea was calmer further from the boat, and

we were able to enjoy the different world that is the Gulf of Thailand. Fish swam around us and beautiful coral grew up from the depths, and I was lost in wonder. If we had been anywhere in the States, I doubt we would have even been allowed in the water under the conditions of the sea that day, and I still marvel at how being so far away from home and what is comfortable lends itself to some sort of bravery—or maybe just irrational thinking.

But I'm grateful for our experience and, to be honest, very glad that we all made it through unscathed.

Koh Samui

After our stay on Koh Phangan, we ferried back over to Koh Samui, where we rented a small villa in a complex called Samui Beach Village. We felt like kings and queens to be staying in an actual house that looked like what we were used to back home, with an indoor kitchen, bathrooms with showers that were not spraying all over the toilet, and soft couches and beds. It was strange, really, to suddenly be surrounded by our usual comforts, because I think we all had become accustomed to the typical Thailand lodging that we had embraced at all of our previous stops.

Samui Beach Village gave us an opportunity to shop at the local markets and cook some of the amazing recipes we had gathered along the way. It was a relaxing and fun few days of cooking, exploring, tearing around on our rented motor scooters, catching crabs and other sea creatures with the kids, and playing. I only needed to gather a few more recipes, and after getting to know the wonderful staff, we arranged a private lesson with Chef Eak, the executive chef at Samui Beach Villas. He came to our villa and proudly showed us several recipes that you will find in this book, including one of my absolute favorites, Deep-Fried Fish with Fried Herbs (page 206).

Our last adventure in the islands was an amazing day trip to An Thong Marine National Park. I did a little research, and from what I read, the best way to experience the marine park was to secure a private boat. The larger tours, it seemed, cram you onto a boat with up to forty other people, put you at the mercy of the tour guide, and force you to go from place to place on a specific schedule. With so many of us to accommodate, this sounded daunting, so we splurged and decided to take advantage of a private tour. The day was unbelievable, and you'll see in the pictures that what we witnessed was true natural beauty at its finest. We ended the tour of the park on a tiny island, swimming in the most beautiful water I had ever seen and playing on soft white sand, lost in the magic of the Gulf of Thailand. I wanted to stay right there forever.

Back to Bangkok, and Returning Home

The last leg of our journey had begun. We headed back to Bangkok for two days before the long, long, long flight home, and interestingly enough, we all were looking forward to the hustle and nuttiness of Bangkok. There is so much excitement and things to see, taste, and do. It's an immediate immersion into Southeast Asian culture, and it's intense with life, flavor, meaning, and wonder. Being in Bangkok makes you feel very small in the universe, and very alive.

Once back in Bangkok, we made sure to explore the backpacker's district known as Khao San Road. This was one of our favorite places, with food and shopping as far as the eye could see. Khao San Road is where we had our final insect-eating encounter, and we bought a bag of crunchy seasoned goodies for the kids to try. It's also where we all tried deep-fried scorpion. Scary, yes, but the crunchy little monster tasted like shrimp. On Khao San Road we enjoyed our last Thai massages, kids and all; picked up final souvenirs for friends and family back home; and ate Thai food until we wanted to burst. We tried to fit some kind of Thai experience into every last minute before heading home.

Mike, America, John and I spent our last evening at Sky Bar, the highest open-air bar in Bangkok (a few scenes from *The Hangover Part II* were filmed there), and ate dinner at the adjoining restaurant, Sirocco. This was by far the most extravagant evening we spent in Thailand, and it was purely for fun and to say we did it. Surprisingly enough, we

spent more on that meal for four people than we typically spent on our street food for nine, and the food we had in the humble places was a thousand times better than the food at the sophisticated and expensive Sirocco. Still, it was an unforgettable evening, and I remember looking down on Bangkok from the top of the world and wishing that our trip did not have to come to an end.

Flying out of Bangkok, we were happy and sad at the same time. I was happy to come back home to Coby, our friends, our pets, and my bed; however, tears streamed down my face as we left. I am crying as I type, remembering our adventures and how I loved the freedom of being lost in a sea of people, swept into a culture so different from ours, unrecognized and yet embraced with Thai smiles from everyone that we met. The Thai culture is accepting yet distant, which is sometimes a welcome reprieve from the intense scrutiny we can face in our Western culture. Thai culture is more concerned about treating others as you should and saving face, not prying. What's private is private, and what you choose to do is your choice. Everyone has a place, a role, a job to be done, and a significant meaning in the world.

That's not to say that all that happens in Thailand is wonderful. Bad things do happen in this country, but then bad things happen everywhere around the world, all the time, and being open to learning about and visiting this amazing place is a big part of helping solve those problems.

I long to return to Thailand, and I look forward to the day that I can again get lost in the land of smiles.

Thank you again to everyone that we met on our journey: I will always remember you.

Recipe Index

Essentials, Condiments, and Curry Pastes

32 Coconut Milk

36 Jasmine Rice

38 Sticky Rice

40 Cauliflower Rice

42 Garlic-Infused Vinegar

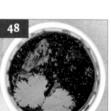
44 Tamarind Paste

46 Toasted Rice Powder

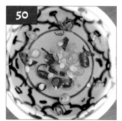
48 Beef Marinade

50 Chile Oil

52 Deep-Fried Garlic

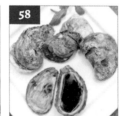
54 Curry Pastes

58 Oyster Sauce

60 Sweet and Sour Sauce

62 Fish Sauce with Chiles

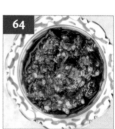
64 Thai Chili Paste

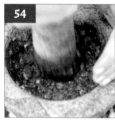
66 Dried Chili Dipping Sauce

68 "Peanut" Sauce

70 Cucumber Relish

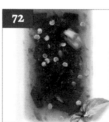
72 Sweet Chili Sauce

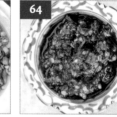

Appetizers and Salads

76
Spring Rolls

78
Leaf Bites

80
Garlic-Fried Prawns

82
Chicken Satay

84
Grilled Pork or Chicken

86
Deep-Fried Chicken
with Creamy Lime Sauce

88
Northern-Style Chili

90
Pork Rinds

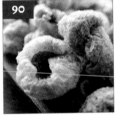
92
Papaya Salad

94
Pomelo Salad

96
Spicy Cucumber Salad

98
Thai Seafood or Ground
Meat Salad

100
Pork Salad with Spicy
Lime Dressing

102
Spicy Snow Mushroom
Salad

104
Spicy Mixed Fruit Salad

106
Spicy Grilled Beef Salad

108
Glass Noodle Salad

110
Green Mango Salad

Fried Rice, Noodles, and Egg Dishes

114

Thai Fried Rice

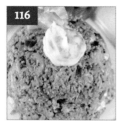
116

Fried Rice with
Pineapple and Prawns

118

Garlic Fried Rice

120

Stir-Fried Rice Noodles

122

Stir-Fried Flat Noodles

124

Deep-Fried Omelet

126

Stuffed Egg Omelet

128

Sweet Chili Eggs

Curries and Soups

132

Red Curry

134

Yellow Curry

136

Green Curry

138

Massaman Curry

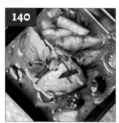
140

Duck Curry with
Fresh Fruit

142

Panaeng Curry

144

Northern-Style Slow-
Cooked Pork

146

Southern Pork with
Yellow Curry

148

Spicy Northern Curry

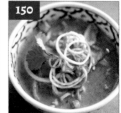
150

Northern-Style Curry

152
Southern Sour Curry

154
Boiled Rice Soup

156
Savory Glass Noodle Soup

158
Sweet and Sour Chicken and Coconut Soup

160
Clear Spicy Soup

162
Creamy Hot and Sour Prawn Soup

164
Shrimp with Pak Miang Leaves in Coconut Milk

166
Sour and Spicy Prawn with Lemongrass Soup

Stir-Fry and Seafood

170
Sweet Basil Leaf Stir-Fry

172
Crab and Yellow Curry Stir-Fry

174
Stir-Fry Fish with Celery

176
Sweet and Sour Stir-Fry

178
Stir-Fried Crispy Pork Belly

180
Stir-Fried Pork with Curry

182
Cashew Nut Stir-Fry

184
Shrimp Stir-Fry with Curry

186
Stir-Fried Chili Shrimp

188
Chicken Fried with Curry

190

Stir-Fried Morning Glory

192

Stir-Fried Pak Miang

194

Stir-Fried Mixed Vegetables

196

Deep-Fried Pork with Pepper and Garlic

198

Indian Curry

200

Deep-Fried Fish with Chu Chee Curry Sauce

202

Deep-Fried Fish Cakes

204

Steamed Fish with Lime and Chili Sauce

206

Deep-Fried Fish with Thai Herbs

208

Fish with Tri-Flavored Sauce

Desserts

212

Pumpkin Custard

214

Crispy Fried Bananas

216

Thai Coconut Pancakes

218

Mango Sticky Rice

220

Bananas in Coconut Milk

Index